The Pictorial History of
FOOTBALL

The Pictorial History of
FOOTBALL

The Pictorial History of
FOOTBALL

CONTENTS

PAGE 1: *The 1928 Olympics, held in Holland, saw Uruguay win the soccer gold medal. Here, the eventual winners dispose of Germany 4-1.*

PAGES 2-3: *Denis Law, of Manchester United, Manchester City and Scotland fame, shoots at goal.*

THESE PAGES: *The 1966 World Cup saw England defeat West Germany in a thrilling and controversial final 4-2.*

Published by Grange Books
An imprint of Books & Toys Ltd
The Grange
Grange Yard
London SE1 3AG

Produced by
Bison Books Ltd
Kimbolton House
117A Fulham Road
London SW3 6RL

Copyright © 1990 Bison Books Ltd

ISBN 1-85627-030-0

Printed in Hong Kong

PART I

Soccer Kicks Off

ORIGINS AND BEGINNINGS

Few games can truly be said to be worldwide. But association football – also commonly known as soccer, to differentiate it first from rugby football, then American football – can be said to have got as close as any. Requiring a spherical ball rather than a specially shaped one, it can be improvised almost anywhere by any number of players. Though a contact sport, it has been played by people of five feet or less, and occasionally those of excessive height or weight. And with the objective simply to score a goal between two posts (or rolled up coats or other markers), its rules are more easily comprehensible than most of its rivals.

So where did the game originate? As with most such questions, there is no easy answer. The Chinese are recorded to have played *tsu chu* – *tsu* meaning to kick and *chu* a stuffed leather ball. The Japanese meanwhile played *kemari*, a game of eight players apiece played on a pitch some 14 metres square, the boundaries marked by four trees – a willow, cherry, pine and maple. The games may in fact be related, since early sporting contact between the countries was recorded. Elsewhere, Mexico justified their double selection as twentieth century World Cup hosts by mixing the skills of football with those of basketball, setting hoops on a wall to form goals for the rival teams to aim at.

The first football in Britain may well have been imported with the Romans when they invaded. Called *harpustum*, a Roman word for 'handball', it was an individual ball game with physical contact very much part and parcel of it, and was developed from the rather more genteel Ancient Greek *episkyros*. The Roman legions may well have played this as they awaited their return to sunnier climes. Back in Italy, the game developed into the sixteenth century *calcio*, with teams of 26 or 27 players apiece, typically wearing green or red colours. These games were often the subject of much money changing hands on the touchline. The rules, *discorsa calcio*, were formalised around 1580.

As the translation of *harpustum* suggests, however, these were games more akin to today's rugby than modern football. Yet the two modern games developed from a common root, only to be divided in nineteenth century England. And, perhaps surprisingly for a game now associated with the working classes, this division and codification of association football took place in the public schools where the monied upper classes sent their children to be educated into young gentlemen.

PAGE 6: *A postcard from 1900 entitled 'Heading the Ball'.*

LEFT: *A relief depicting a Greek youth showing off his skills.*

LEFT: Calcio, *a Renaissance form of soccer played between retainers of the leading Florentine families.*

RIGHT: *An early example of a soccer match, probably before 1700.*

LEFT: *Inflating the ball before the match begins, a seventeenth century scene.*

9

FOOTBALL IN BRITAIN

Britain may not have invented association football, but it can certainly claim to have developed and formalised the rules which, by and large, still hold sway the world over. Yet prior to its adoption by the gentry in the nineteenth century the game enjoyed a reputation as the sport of hooligans and rabble-rousers. And little wonder, with the participants in the average game outnumbering the crowds at many English Third and Fouth Division games today. Several fixtures in the early history of football attained the status of annual rituals, being recorded in written works and art. The Shrove Tuesday contest at Ashbourne, Derbyshire, celebrates one of the earliest recorded indigenous football games. With one half of the town pitted against the other (what price Merseyside or Manchester?), the goals are the parish church at one end and the gates of Ashbourne Hall at the other. This bizarre 'fixture' was first recorded in the year AD 217, and continues to this day.

Even then, the game had spread far and wide: Dorset's Corfe Castle and Scone in Scotland were among other venues where an annual Shrove Tuesday fixture was observed. At Chester, a leather ball was introduced (appropriately courtesy of the town's cobblers), the City Hall and the hall at Rodehoe being the goals for the game. Few, however, played on pitches such as the one recorded in Cornwall in 1602, whose goals were three to four miles apart and the teams were each comprised of the menfolk of two or three neighbouring parishes. London was at the forefront of these 'mob football' games, perhaps the only ones where the hooligans took an active part! The meat market at Smithfield was a favoured venue for the apprentices to gather in numbers up to 500-strong, while Cheapside, Covent Garden and the genteel suburb of Kingston Upon Thames were among the other noted venues.

With few – if any – rules prevailing and uncontrollable numbers of players in action, the risk of permanent injury was high. Scores could be (and doubtless were) settled during the course of such games, and there was an inevitable backlash from authority. Kings, the clergy, the womenfolk, even the Puritans, all attempted to have the game banned . . . without success. Football has always had its critics. The game has often been seen as a source of national pride and a peaceful way of settling scores. In 1365, however, King Edward III had exactly the opposite situation on his hands when it became apparent his soldiers would rather play football than fight. The inevitable ban is said to have improved their archery, but failed to stamp out the game. Indeed, a contemporary carving in Gloucester Cathedral, no less, shows two fourteenth century footballers vying for possession – an indication that the game was nearing acceptablility.

When Cambridge University introduced it into their curriculum at the turn of the seventeenth century, even its detractors had to reconsider. But with a welter of different rules proliferating, these games were strictly intramural affairs. With the advent of the Industrial Revolution, few of the downtrodden working classes had the time or energy to pursue such a physically demanding sport – and football passed into the hands of the leisured upper classes. Each public school, it seemed, had its own special set of rules, often tailored to conform to the surface on which the game was played. At Charterhouse, where the stony cloisters provided the pitch for 20 players a side, the ball was played by feet alone; at Rugby, handling (but not running in possession) was positively encouraged. Harrow played a recognisable form of today's game on grass, 11 players making up a team, while Winchester's goals extended the entire length of the goal line, rather like rugby's try line today.

It was inevitable that this situation would not last. The catalyst for change and standardisation was William Webb Ellis's legendary dash with the ball in 1823 that eventually gave rise to the game of rugby. This form of football broke ranks with soccer in 1848, when a 14-man committee at Cambridge University defined the game as permitting handling only to control the ball. Further rules then

BELOW: *An eighteenth century rendition of an early soccer match in the Strand, London.*

BOTTOM: *Mob football in London – a match in Crowe Street in 1721. The players' expressions attest to the risk of physical injury.*

ABOVE RIGHT: *The famous fourteenth century misericord from Gloucester Cathedral, a sign of the game's increasing acceptance.*

BELOW RIGHT: *Harrow was one of the English public schools where football developed into the game we know today.*

BOTTOM RIGHT: *Eton's first XI of 1865. By this stage, an 11-man team had become standard.*

BOTTOM, FAR RIGHT: *An unidentified school team from 1866 pose with their trophy.*

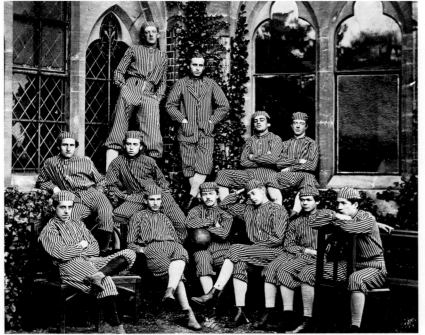

decided upon stated that the goals should consist of two posts. Fouls were defined as tripping, kicking or holding, and an offside rule insisting on three men between the passer and the opposing goal was instituted. Football had arrived, and when the Sheffield Cricket Club permitted matches to be played on their Bramall Lane pitch in the late 1850s, it seemed it almost had respectability. Sheffield could thus claim to be Britain's oldest football club. Today they continue that proud tradition, although firmly in the shadow of League giants Wednesday and United. Their players emanated from the city's Old Collegiate School. Games against local rivals such as Hallam (formed 1857) attracted 600 spectators, while their 1904 Amateur Cup win remains their greatest achievement.

Such organisation was by no means confined to the North. The Blackheath Club formed in Kent in 1857, while others formed in the 1850s included Hampstead Heathens (playing, of course, on London's Hampstead Heath). The Old Harrovians were ex-pupils of Harrow School, while other Harrow old boys founded Wanderers, originally named Forest Football Club after their ground in Epping Forest near Snaresbrook. Notts County, established in 1862, were the first of the current Football League clubs to be founded. With such grassroots activity flourishing, the way was clear for an association of these teams to be formed.

ASSOCIATION FOOTBALL

The face of football has never been changed quite so radically as on 26 October 1863 when 11 southern English clubs each sent representatives to London's Freemason's Tavern in the west central district of Holborn. Their intent was to thrash out a commonly acceptable form of rules by which the game of football could be played. They adopted the following resolution: 'That it is advisable that a football association should be formed for the purpose of settling a code of rules for the regulation of the game of football.' An annual general meeting was set for the last week in September (thus setting the beginning of the traditional football season). All those clubs which were of at least a year's standing could send two representatives if their one guinea subscription was fully paid up. Not all those present, however, could give total backing to the movement. The Charterhouse representative, for instance, agreed with the broad aims of the association but felt he had to wait to gauge the reaction of the other 'great schools' before giving up their own brand of the game. Harrow, too, were initially unwilling to change their home-grown rules.

The actual rules themselves were agreed by early December – and, fortunately for the reluctant Harrow representative, they were based on that school's understanding of how the game was played. Prior to this, however, impassioned discussion had led to the resignation of Rugby from the association, not on the issue of handling but on the question of 'hacking' or physically kicking opponents. The Rugby Football Union was formed in 1871 by those for whom handling and hacking held no fears. The rules agreed by the FA included the maximum length and breadth of the pitch, the procedures for kicking off, defined a goal, throw-in and offside. Corners were effectively free kicks, taken 15 yards from the goal line opposite where the ball went out of play. The rugby tactic of 'making a mark' (catching the ball and making a mark with the heel to claim a free kick) remained. Passing the ball by hand was permitted if caught 'fairly or on the first bounce'. Yet even though nails, iron plates and *gutta percha* (whatever *that* might be) were banned from footwear, the rules were strangely non-specific in such matters as number of players, the penalty for foul play or even the shape of the ball. Such matters were deemed to be decided by agreement between the captains.

Rudimentary and incomplete as these rules were in themselves, they had the immediate effect of stimulating competition. An annual New Year fixture between Sheffield and Nottingham was inaugurated on 2 January 1865, Nottingham (now Notts County), the oldest current League club having been founded two years earlier. Sheffield ventured to London in the following year, but having won the first Nottingham fixture they then found themselves at the wrong end of a 4-0 scoreline. In 1865, Nottingham Forest were formed, and the first 'derby' game against local rivals County followed. Chesterfield (1866) and Stoke (1867) were next to join, and the game spread, no longer the exclusive preserve of the public schools yet by no means a working class pastime. A crucial rule re-

laxed in 1867 was the provision that players in front of the ball were offside, thus reducing passing movements to lateral or backward directions. No wonder few goals were scored! This rule change took time to effect the pattern of play, which depended largely on individuals dribbling their way into a scoring position. Sheffield's game in London in 1866 had enabled the FA to observe their rules at close quarters. As a result, handling and catching the ball were soon abolished (save for the goalkeeper) and a tape was stretched between the posts (Sheffield's bar was introduced in 1882). But it was contact with the Scots who had developed their game well away from public school influence that was to rapidly broaden football's horizons.

The first FA Cup Final was contested in 1872, before 2000 paying spectators, by Wanderers and Royal Engineers, the latter hot favourites. Injury, however, played a crucial part as it so often did in these pre-substitute days, and a broken collarbone sustained in the first few minutes by an Engineers player effectively put them at a disadvantage. Wanderers managed just one goal, but it was enough. This was scored by one AH Chequer, a pseudonym used by MP Betts to signify he had been a member of the Harrow Chequers old boys' team scheduled to face Wanderers in the first round. The team had scratched, hence Betts was not cup-tied and ended up playing for his intended opponents!

The FA Cup was clearly the start of something big. Within a matter of a few years, all clubs vied to take part – and by doing so accepted the FA rules of football which remain the basis by which the game is played throughout the world today. The dominant teams in the Cup's first years were the 'Gentlemen' or southerners, with Old Etonians (6), Wanderers (5), Royal Engineers and Oxford University (both 4) clocking up most final appearances in the first dozen. Outside this Big Four, only four other sides managed to reach the final at all – the Blackburns Olympic and Rovers, Old Carthusians and Clapham Rovers. Wanderers notched the greatest number of wins, emerging victorious in all five of their FA Cup appearances.

One of their finals, in 1873, saw them play just one game to win. This was the only season in which the FA Challenge Cup, to give it its full name, was played as a true challenge, the other teams playing each other for the right to throw down the gauntlet. Not unsurprisingly, Oxford University, the eventual challengers, were somewhat more fatigued than their opponents and succumbed 2-0, unusually choosing to play without a goalkeeper. Scottish team Queen's Park had withdrawn from the semi-final due to problems raising travel expenses, a decision that led directly to the formation of the Scottish FA.

Wanderers won the Cup outright after what remains one of only two hat-tricks of wins, between 1876 and 1878. The Cup was, however, returned to the Football Association on condition that no club could subsequently win it outright. Wanderers' main rivals in the 1870s were the Royal Engineers, who lost only twice (both Cup Finals, in 1872 and 1874) in their 86 matches between 1871 and 1875. Their Major Marindin was later FA President, and after appearing in two losing FA Cup Finals, was to referee a further eight.

BELOW LEFT: *Hacking (kicking opponents) was swiftly outlawed by the newly formed Football Association in 1863.*

BELOW: *This 1888 game illustrates the original form of crossbar – a tape stretched between the posts to limit the height of the goal.*

PLAYING THE GAME (1)

By the time the Football Association was formed in 1863, the teams had settled to 11 players apiece – and, with the obvious and notable exception of Rugby, it was accepted that only one player on either side, the goalkeeper, could handle the ball. As we will observe shortly, however, local variations still existed. Corner kicks from the intersection of touch and goal line were generally introduced in 1872, although the Sheffield clubs had been using these for four years or so previously. Wing-halves typically fulfilled the corner-kicking responsibilities, handing over to wing-forwards around the turn of the century. As with children's playground football today, everyone wanted to be an attacker: thus the goalkeeper was typically covered by, at most, two defenders. Players bunched into thirds of the field, leaving wide open spaces unattended.

It was the Scots who first discovered the opportunities this offered, and their emphasis on team play saw them advance apace. They were also assisted by playing to consistent rules. The 5-3-2 formation evolved, with three of the forwards now dropping deeper as half-backs to provide an extra line of defence where necessary; the centre-half acted as the supply route to the front line. This 'pyramid' style of play was employed by the double-winning Preston team in the League's first season, and their double success spoke for itself.

One major problem with the offside rule was exploited by Newcastle's Billy McCracken. He would move forward to play his opponents offside, knowing that there was still a covering defender as well as the goalkeeper to foil the attacker even if he mistimed his run – which was not often. Other teams followed suit, and the result was games where the team in possession found themselves stopped at the half-way line. The balance was quite clearly wrong, and had to be tilted in favour of enterprising play. Not surprisingly in view of past events, this was at the Scots' insistence. The new law simply removed a defending player from the equation. Now two players had to be between the man in possession and his opponents' goal line when the ball was played – a situation that left the defenders far less margin for error. Few were willing to risk exposing their goalkeeper, and those that did often paid the penalty. Statistically speaking, the change was an immediate success. In the season following the law change, the goal tally for the League's divisions rose from 4700 to 6373.

Penalties were introduced in September 1891 as a result of an incident in the previous season, during an FA Cup quarter final between Notts County and Stoke at Trent Bridge. County's Hendry produced an acrobatic goalkeeping save – unfortunately, however, he was the left-back. A free kick was awarded on the goal line, but goalkeeper Toone saved the point-blank shot. Since County's 1-0 win meant they reached the semi-final and later the final, a public outcry provoked a change in the laws. By cruel irony, Stoke were also put at a disadvantage the following season when Aston Villa's goalkeeper kicked the ball out of the ground in disgust when Stoke were awarded a penalty. Since only two minutes remained on the referee's watch, there was insufficient time to retrieve the ball and Stoke, again losing 1-0, were denied the chance to save the game. Subsequent changes decreed that time should be added on to enable the penalty to be taken even if normal time had elapsed, while in 1892 the rules stated that a player could kick the ball only once before it had to be touched by another. This prevented the ball being dribbled into goal from the spot.

While football was changing its rules and regulations, playing kit was undergoing its own metamorphosis. In the 1870s, for instance, a match programme was essential for player identification, the colour of stockings or cap being the only differentiating feature between players on the same team. Although numbering was not introduced until 1933, caps had long since fallen into disuse. The first 30 years of the Football League had seen little or no experimentation in terms of team formation, but all that was soon to change.

The last side to win with the old-fashioned pyramid or 'W' formation (with the centre-half as playmaker rather than central stopper) was the Huddersfield team, inspired on the pitch by centre-half Wilson and off by the legendary Herbert Chapman, that took a hat-trick of championships from 1924-26. It was Chapman himself, however, who was to inspire the next significant revolution in British – and world – football.

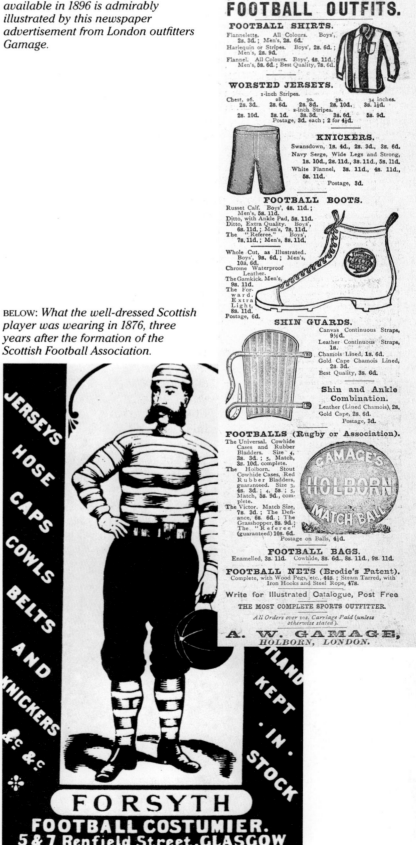

RIGHT: *The football equipment available in 1896 is admirably illustrated by this newspaper advertisement from London outfitters Gamage.*

BELOW: *What the well-dressed Scottish player was wearing in 1876, three years after the formation of the Scottish Football Association.*

GENTLEMEN AND PLAYERS

Stimulated by the 1866 game with Sheffield, the London-based Football Association determined to expand the game's influence into a wider area. Sheffield themselves joined in 1867, and other teams from all points of the compass were quick to follow suit. The amazing expansion of the 1870s was due primarily to the effort of one Charles Alcock, elected at the tender age of 28 as Secretary of the Association. He devised the idea of international competition, inaugurating the annual England-Scotland fixture that survives to this day. His *modus operandi* was to address the readers of the *Glasgow Herald*, advising them that the FA was to stage an international match at Kennington Oval, home of Surrey Cricket Club, on 19 November. Representatives were invited.

Captain of the team that emerged from this public appeal was Robert Smith, one of the three brothers instrumental in the formation of Queen's Park FC and now resident in London. His team, which lost 1-0 in the fixture, was composed entirely of Scots living south of the border (the reaction of the *Glasgow Herald*'s readership remains unrecorded), but the stage had been set for three repeat encounters, in which the best Scotland could manage was a single 1-1 draw. The balance of power was to shift noticeably, however, with the first international on Scottish soil (a goalless draw at the West of Scotland Cricket Club at Partick on 30 November 1872), and one of the most bitterly-disputed fixtures in the history of football was well and truly born. Meanwhile, Alcock had devised the ideal method of encouraging competitive play: the Football Association Cup, purchased for the princely sum of £20. Fifteen clubs entered for the 1871-72 competition, though one – Donington Grammar School in Lincolnshire – withdrew without playing a game. Queen's Park, who contributed a guinea to the cost of the trophy, were lucky enough to draw Donington – then, thanks to a lopsided draw, contest the semi-finals without having had to play a single qualifying game.

Their semi-final against Wanderers (the team of which Alcock was secretary, and formerly known as Forest) was played in London, as indeed were all semis and finals for the first years. The two teams could not break the goalless deadlock, and with extra time and penalty shootouts not yet devised, the Scots withdrew, being unable to manage the 800-mile round trip to Glasgow and back for the replay.

The demise of Wanderers as strongest of the Gentlemen teams was mirrored by the rise of the public schools' 'old boy' teams. Two Old Etonians' victories over them in 1878-79 and 1879-80 seem to have marked the turning of the tide. Their most famous player Arthur (later Lord) Kinnaird, a future FA President, chose to play for his old school rather than the team he'd represented previously. This was a significant loss, for Kinnaird was clearly the outstanding player of the age. He won five Cup winners medals, as well as one cap for Scotland. After retiring from playing, he served as FA President for some 33 years. A season after the second defeat, Wanderers threw in the towel and retired from competitive football completely. It may be as well that they did, for the game was about to be taken over by the 'professors', professional footballers from Scotland who lent their talents to such northern teams as Darwen, Sheffield Wednesday and Bolton. Professionalism reflected the industrial nature of the North, where leisure time was at a premium. The match that signified the end of the Gentlemen's monopoly was the Cup Final of 1882 when Blackburn became the first northern club to make it to the last stage of the contest. They were unlucky to lose 1-0 to Old Etonians, and indeed had been tipped to win. Their run of 31 wins and four draws is the longest ever unbeaten sequence in English first-class football. Lord Kinnaird was the Etonians' captain, and he created history by standing on his head after receiving the Cup. The competition was about to be turned upside down, too: Old Etonians were the last amateur club to win the trophy, and no southern team was to write their name on it before the end of the century.

Three public parks existed in Glasgow. The keenest footballers gathered at Queen's Park, so it was not surprising that the leading club should bear that name. Queen's Park contested the FA Cup keenly until the SFA outlawed participation in 1887. They reached the final twice, in 1884 and 1885: their opponents in each case were Blackburn Rovers, the scores 2-1 and 2-0. The first game was contentious in that referee Major Marindin disallowed two Queen's Park goals for offside, due to confusion about which offside rule was being played. Blackburn went on to emulate Wanderers in winning the Cup three times in consecutive years, triumphing over West Bromwich after a replay. Their captain Jimmy Brown created a record for himself in scoring in each of the three games. And though they could not now win the Cup in perpetuity, Blackburn returned to win again in 1890 and 1891. The professionals had well and truly taken over.

BELOW: *England, in the white strip, head for goal in their fixture against Scotland in 1879. They won by five goals to four.*

BELOW LEFT: *Blackburn Rovers win their second consecutive FA Cup, this time against Notts County at London's Kennington Oval in 1891.*

THE LEAGUE TAKES OFF

It seems far fetched to say the least, but the founder of the English Football League was a Scotsman – a man, moreover, who never played a game of first-class football in his entire life. Perthshire gentleman William McGregor was the prime mover behind two meetings held in the spring of 1888 in London and Manchester involving the 12 football clubs who were to become the League's founder members. The London meeting took place on 22 March 1888 at Anderton's Hotel in London, on the eve of that year's Cup Final. The clubs' revenue depended on a good Cup run: an early exit could be financially disastrous, while postponements of friendly games due to Cup replays often meant fixtures were not fulfilled, resulting in an understandable lack of commitment from many spectators. Matters were completed on 17 April at the Royal Hotel in Manchester.

Curiously, McGregor originally thought the name Football League would be confused with the politically motivated Irish Land League, but that, by majority vote, was the name selected for this new competition that guaranteed fixtures and revenue for the country's top dozen teams. Geographically speaking, these clubs were split equally between the North and the Midlands; the South of England remained a stronghold of the amateur game, and no professional football of note was played there.

Preston North End were the first champions in the season 1888-89, with Aston Villa runners-up. So dominant were they, in fact, that they achieved the League and Cup double. What wrote their name into the record books, however, was the fact that they were undefeated in the League (and did not concede a Cup goal) – a record that seems likely never to be broken, given the minimum of 44 fixtures it would now take a First Division club to achieve the same feat. Their record in that first season bears repeating. Playing 22 matches, home and away, they won 18 and drew four. Their goals for were 74, goals against 15 – and as previously mentioned their Cup win was achieved with a totally clean sheet. The team was predominantly Scottish, with the England centre-forward John Goodall the star 'foreigner'.

Preston won the League the following year also, despite four defeats, with Everton second – a foretaste of things to come, since the positions were reversed in the 1890-91 season. Preston claimed the runners-up spot for three seasons running, underlining their claim to be the first major force in League football. That last season saw the 12 founder members become 14 with the addition of Stoke and Darwen.

The original intention was that Football League points should be awarded solely for wins. But after 10 weeks of the first season, this was amended to make drawn games yield one point apiece as compared to two points for a win – a system that remained in operation until 1981-82, when the proliferation of goalless draws encouraged the League to improve the points for a win to three.

ABOVE: *Preston centre-forward John Goodall, one of the outstanding players in Britain's first legendary league team.*

LEFT: *Preston North End, the first Football League winners in the season 1888-89. The side also took the FA Cup without conceding a goal.*

LANCASHIRE LEADS

'Proud' Preston's mantle was donned in the 1890s by Sunderland, who took the League title in the seasons 1891-92, 1892-93 and again in 1894-95, having finished second to Aston Villa in the intervening season. Their success stoked the fires of football fervour in the Northeast, where the industrial base provided by shipbuilding supplied both the men to play football and the crowds to watch. The team also included a Scots contingent, drawn southwards across the border in search of fame and fortune. One of these, goalkeeper Ned Doig, played against West Bromwich on 20 September 1890 before his transfer from Arbroath had been formally registered, costing his new club two points. He proved a worthwhile buy in the long term, however. In seven seasons, the team were beaten only once at Roker Park. Sunderland were known as the 'Team of All the Talents'. In 1892-93, their first championship campaign, they topped 100 goals for the first time in League history, being assisted by the expansion of the division to 16 clubs. This feat was not to be equalled until the interwar years when West Bromwich notched 104 goals in a 22-club division. Sunderland had not, in fact, been one of the founding 12, but their history was impressive enough. Added to the League strength in 1890 when Stoke temporarily dropped out, they retained their First Division place until 1958. By then, they had added another three championships to their 1890s successes.

Aston Villa had been first to challenge the northern supremacy. As previously noted, they won in 1893-94, and were from 1895-96 to monopolise the title for the five seasons to the end of the century, save a single win (in 1897-98) by Sheffield United The latter had joined the League in 1893, a year after their city rivals Wednesday.

The League had added a 12-strong Second Division for the season 1892-93, simultaneously adding a further two teams to the First. The lower echelon had previously been known as the Football Alliance, a competition set up in 1889 by a group of non-League teams which had shown its collective class by drawing in a representative match with a League XI. The promotion and relegation issues were to be settled by a series of three test matches, these pitting Second Division champions against the bottom First Division club, runners-up against second from bottom and third-placed against the third from bottom. As a result Sheffield United and Darwen were promoted, with Notts County – one of the founding 12 – relegated.

This arrangement was, of course, all but duplicated in the 1980s when play-offs were introduced, initially with the purpose of reducing the size of the First Division but subsequently retained to add excitement to the end-of-season action. In 1892-93, however,

Birmingham Small Heath could consider themselves unlucky in having topped the lower division yet missing out on promotion, there being then no automatic place. The system was dispensed with after an 1898 fixture between Stoke and Burnley which ended in a goalless draw – coincidentally or otherwise a result that kept both clubs in the top flight. Thereafter, an automatic two up/two down system of promotion and relegation was instituted. This was modified to three-up, three-down in 1973-74, the third place being made the subject of a play-off in 1986-87. The new division had failed to admit a single club from the South: that had to wait until the election of Woolwich Arsenal to the Second Division in 1893. By 1894-95 there were 16 clubs in each division.

The League and Cup double has remained a cherished dream for First Division clubs: only one team managed to repeat Preston's inaugural feat before the end of the century. Aston Villa achieved the distinction in 1897 as part of the four championships in five seasons that rounded off the decade and indeed the century. The magnitude of their feat is underlined by the fact that the runners-up Sheffield United trailed a full 11 points behind, and that their status as the second double winners endured for fully 64 years until the Spurs team of 1960-61. Having secured the League title some while before the end of the season must have helped Villa somewhat, but the ease of their first round despatch of Newcastle United, 5-0, was not matched by their third-round jitters against Preston. No longer quite the force they were, North End nevertheless took Villa to a third game before succumbing by the narrowest of 3-2 margins. Up until the replay, Villa had profited from home advantage throughout the Cup.

BELOW: *A clash of heads in the 1895 FA Cup Final between Aston Villa and West Bromwich.*

BELOW LEFT: *South London's Crystal Palace was the venue for 1897's Cup Final in which Aston Villa beat Everton 3-2.*

Beating Liverpool with ease 3-0 in the semi-final, Villa faced their Merseyside rivals at Crystal Palace, defeating them 3-2 to add the Cup to the prize already secured. One of the powerhouses of this team was half-back John Reynolds, an international for both England and Ireland (though born in Blackburn). Villa had won the Cup two years earlier, defeating West Bromwich by a single goal at the first Crystal Palace final. The Cup won in double year was a different one since, after lending it to sports outfitter William Shillcock for display in his window, they never saw it again. The £25 which Villa were fined for this misdemeanour paid for a new trophy. A newspaper interview with an 83-year-old, Harry Burge, in 1958 claimed the Cup was melted down to manufacture forged coin.

The FA Cup provided surprises in the following two years. In 1900, non-League Southampton battled to the final before being dispatched in no uncertain fashion, 4-0, by Bury of the First Division. The following year, however, saw even more of a shock when Tottenham Hotspur became the first – and still the only – non-League club to win the Cup since 1888. They took two games to defeat Sheffield United, runners-up in the League the season before but 14th out of 18th that year despite the stopping skills of the legendary 21-stone goalkeeper 'Fatty' Foulke. A replay at Burnden Park, Bolton, was required to settle matters 3-1 after a 2-2 draw at Crystal Palace. Centre-forward Sandy Brown also set a record by scoring in every round of the competition – a record total of 15 goals that has yet to be surpassed. He notched three of these in the finals, including both Spurs' strikes in the original game. Spurs were then members of the Southern League and remained outside the League until 1908: their first season in the Second Division saw them finish second and obtain promotion. Interestingly, their Cup-winning team had contained 11 Northerners.

BOTTOM: *First Division Bury face non-League Southampton in the 1900 FA Cup Final.*

RIGHT: *An artist's impression of the scenes at the 1902 Cup Final between Sheffield United and Southampton.*

BELOW: *Sheffield United goalkeeper 'Fatty' Foulke, whose weight was variously estimated at between 21 and 26 stones.*

NORTH OF THE BORDER

One of the main reasons the game of football took off in Scotland in preference to rugby may well be the fact that well-grassed areas were few and far between, especially in the Scottish lowlands. Soccer could be – and frequently was – improvised anywhere and everywhere. On 9 July 1867 the Queen's Park Football Club was founded in Glasgow, where there were only three parks to alleviate the need to play on cobbles. The club was founded at 3 Eglinton Terrace, Glasgow, three brothers named Smith being among those present. One, Robert, was soon to be appointed Scotland's first national captain. Those he consorted with on this occasion included soccer enthusiasts, YMCA members and a number of Highland Games specialists who all used the park whose name they adopted. First games were strictly intramural, the members splitting into north and south of the River Clyde. As the game grew in popularity elsewhere, competitive games were introduced, the first of these being in August 1868 against a club named Thistle.

Over the three years following their formation, Queen's Park were to attract Scotland's best players to their ranks, but until the establishment of international matches with England, they had little contact with the Football Association. They joined the FA to take part in the first FA Cup competitions, and were to remain members for over a decade until the newly-formed Scottish Football Association outlawed participation in 1887. They reached the final twice, in 1884 and 1885. Their opponents in each case were Blackburn Rovers, the scores 2-1 and 2-0. Queen's Park's total dominance of football north of the border can be gauged by the fact that all but two of the team that met England in the first international on Scottish soil on 30 November 1872 were from the club. The two that were not, two of the Smith brothers, were both ex-members now living in London. The gate receipts from the match, a goalless draw, were £200, with the 4000 spectators each charged one shilling admission. Such untold riches encouraged Queen's Park to seek larger accommodation, which became available in the shape of Hampden Park. This is still the home of Queen's Park FC and the venue at which Scotland's international matches are played.

It was obvious that forming a Scottish equivalent to the English FA would stimulate competition for places in the national side, while playing teams nearer home would make life a lot easier for Queen's Park. If proof were needed, one only had to recall that in 1872 and 1873, the first two years of the FA Cup, the Scots had been obliged to scratch at the semi-final stage (the first time after forcing a draw) through lack of funds. Thus it was that 1873 saw the formation of the eight-team Scottish FA. Seven founder members agreed to accept the rules by which Queen's Park played, since the Glasgow club had always believed itself superior to all other Scots teams of whatever level. Of those eight founder members, only Queen's Park and Kilmarnock survive today: the others, for the record, were Clydesdale, Vale of Leven, Third Lanark, Dumbreck, Eastern and Granville. Such was Queen's Park's continuing superiority, however, that it was not until 16 January 1875 that an opponent even managed to score against them, the team in question being Vale of Leven. Elsewhere, standards were equally uneven: the legendary 36-0 win by Arbroath against Bon Accord in 1885 still stands as the record British first-class football score.

As with Queen's Park, the clubs affiliated to the Scottish FA could, in the early years, compete against English clubs or even be members of both English and Scottish bodies. This was, however, soon to change, the catalyst being the advent of professionalism in England. The Scottish FA chose to bar 68 Scots playing south of the border regarding professionalism as 'evil'. Queen's Park, who today remain the only Scottish League club to have amateur status, were in the forefront of this crusade. Clashes in the 1886-87 FA Cup exacerbated the situation, and Rangers, who went out to Aston Villa in the semi-final held at Crewe, were to be the last Scottish club to venture south.

International matches, of course, continued, with Scotland having by far the upper hand, notching seven wins and two draws in the 11 fixtures since that first Glasgow game. This dominance owed much to Queen's Park's players reproducing club form for their country – as indeed one would expect when the players concerned made up the majority of the team. England selected mainly from top amateur club the Corinthians, ensuring that the taint of professionalism was not felt in this fixture for some time.

The SFA edict that clubs should not belong to any other national organisation nor compete in their competitions meant a Scottish League was desperately needed. Such a body was formed in 1890 – and was, as one would expect, initially proudly amateur. Dumbarton and Rangers shared the first championship, drawing in a playoff game – the only such occasion in the history of the League. Dumbarton emerged to take the title outright the following season. The inevitable quickening of the southwards migration from the all-amateur Scottish game by the most gifted players led to another rash of expulsions. The annual internationals were proving something of a headache, however, since Scotland refused to pick the 'exiles' and inevitably suffered for their pains at the hands of the British professionals. A 5-2 drubbing in 1893 at Richmond was the turning point – and when Celtic, that year's champions, moved a motion to accept professionalism in the Scottish League the old guard was routed. Queen's Park, who had not joined the League, found it impossible to maintain their leading position on an amateur basis. Although they beat champions Celtic to take the 1893 Scottish Cup, it was a pyrrhic victory, and despite swallowing their pride and joining the League in 1899 they were never to scale such heights again. They remain amateurs to this day.

The 1893 team to play England was divided 5-4 between Queen's Park – the team of the past – and Celtic, one of the two teams of the future. Even though the Scottish League grew swiftly – after its first season it could claim the affiliation of 64 clubs in associated leagues – it was thenceforth to be dominated by the two Glasgow clubs, Rangers and Celtic. The 'Old Firm', as they became known, carved up the championship to such an extent that their domination was broken only 13 times by outside clubs between the advent of professionalism in 1893-94 and the introduction of a new three-division system in 1974. A Second Division was established in 1893, although promotion and relegation between the two divisions was far from automatic. This was not to be resolved until these teams, disenchanted by the old boys network, withdrew to form an unrecognised Central League.

BELOW: *The first known photograph of Glasgow Celtic FC, who then wore white shirts with green collars rather than the green and white hoops they sport today.*

SOCCER'S GOLDEN AGE

The first decade of the twentieth century came to be known in Britain as soccer's 'Golden Age', with attendances booming due to a style of play based on the Scottish short-passing game. Newcastle United inhabited the upper echelons of the League at this point: their achievements stopped short of total domination yet were noteworthy in themselves. They first stood on the threshold of the double in 1905, when a 0-2 Cup Final reverse against Aston Villa dashed their hopes of adding it to the League Championship. In 1906 they could only finish fourth, running up in the Cup again to Everton. In 1907 came another championship win, though suffering early Cup defeat against non-League opposition. 1908 saw a repeat of 1906, losing 3-1 to Wolves. The League followed the year after and in 1910 they finally won the coveted Cup.

Their victory over Barnsley by a 2-0 score at Goodison Park after a 1-1 draw at Crystal Palace seemed to confirm the popular theory that they found it hard to compete away from their own St James's Park – Crystal Palace's lush turf being one reason put forward. In 1911 the form book proved true again, when they lost to Bradford City after a replay – at least they could claim to be improving by not losing first time! With five finals and three Championships in seven seasons, they could consider themselves unlucky not to have done the double. Their playmaker was Scots half-back Peter McWilliam, while the cunning defensive play of Irishman Billy McCracken and his defensive partner Hudspeth is covered elsewhere in discussion

ABOVE: *The Wolverhampton team who took the Cup in 1908 when Newcastle once again failed at the final hurdle.*

LEFT: *The Newcastle United team of the early 1900s with full-back McCracken first left and half-back McWilliam third left in top row.*

BOTTOM LEFT: *Aston Villa deny Newcastle the double with a 2-0 Cup Final victory in 1905.*

BELOW: *Newcastle concede their first goal of the game. Note the goalkeeper (in cap) wears the same shirt as his team mates.*

RIGHT AND ABOVE RIGHT: *Billy McCracken, who applied the offside rule so effectively the Football League decided to change it in 1925.*

of the offside rule they used so often to their advantage. So parsimonious was their defence, however, that their 1909 League win had been secured with just 65 'goals for', thanks to a miserly total of 41 against.

The FA Cup venue had settled at the Palace in 1895 after much experiment. It had moved northwards from the Oval, which could accommodate no more than 25,000, to Fallowfield, Manchester (disastrously, 1893) and Goodison Park, Merseyside (more successfully in 1894) before a permanent venue was set at Crystal Palace, where the fixture resided from 1895 to the outbreak of World War I. Crowds approached 100,000, a figure achieved in 1905 when Aston Villa beat Newcastle United in the latter's first double attempt. This was only the second time a match had attracted this figure, the first being 1901 when 114,815 attended. The Football Association introduced extra time in 1913 as a method to decide the destination of the Cup at the first attempt: it proved effective, replays proving unnecessary until 1970.

In the League, Aston Villa had taken two championships at the end of the decade (and century), but apart from another double by Sheffield Wednesday (in 1902-04 inclusive) the title changed hands with surprising regularity. Oldham nearly capped their brief period in the top flight with a championship win, losing out in the final game of the 1914-15 season, the last before war halted competition. Lancashire was more successful in the shape of Blackburn, whose team of 1911-14 won two championships in 1912 and 1914, filling homely Ewood Park more weeks than not. Their captain was the influential Bob Crompton. Manchester United won Championships in 1908 and 1911. 1909 nearly saw the League suspended due to a players strike in favour of the Football Players and Trainers Union, recognising the working class backgrounds from which most of the players now emerged. Despite this effective show of solidarity, it was to be 50 years and more before a player challenged the concept of a maximum wage, decided upon as far back as 1901.

W. Mc CRACKEN.

RIGHT: *Supporters of Newcastle and Everton congregate in London on the day of the game, April 1906.*

21

PART II

The World Game

1919-39

NATIONAL AND INTERNATIONAL

England, Scotland, Wales and Northern Ireland together comprise the Home Countries. Despite constant agitation by pressure groups within FIFA, they have retained their separate national identities and have competed in international football, sometimes against each other. The four have only reached the final stages of the World Cup on a single occasion, in 1958, but there are those who believe a Great Britain team would be fairer. There are also those who believe it would be more successful. The Home International tournament, a round robin between the four countries, was founded in 1883-84 and, until its demise in 1984, was world football's oldest international series. Scotland dominated the scene for its first four years, then sharing with England in 1885-86 as the full impact of professionalism began to be felt.

Football was now establishing a firm foothold outside the United Kingdom, especially in countries with no long-established national game. Denmark, for instance, had entered a team in the 1908 Olympics, staged in London, and at that time represented the only threat to Great Britain's supremacy (unlike the World Cup, the Home Countries joined forces to produce an amateur Olympic team). The Danes finished runners-up in 1908 and 1912, proving their right to the silver medal by vanquishing France 17-1. Denmark could trace their progress back to the English Football Club formed in Copenhagen in 1879, the first of several clubs to make up the Danish FA. Elsewhere, France, Switzerland and Belgium all benefited from the influence of British enthusiasts taking their beloved game overseas. Standard AC in Paris (1892), St Gallen FC in Switzerland (1879) and Antwerp in Belgium (1880) were early outposts where British influence can be traced. The first president of Austria's Football Association was MD Nicholson, a travel agent and a Cup winner with West Bromwich Albion in 1892. Germany adopted Football Association rules in about 1870, and five years later a team from Oxford University toured the country, stimulating a number of universities to take up the game. Portugal's capital, Lisbon, saw activity in 1870

Continental Fußballblase

when English expatriates began to play. A club was formed five years later and the game went national in 1893.

The result of such activity was logical enough – the formation of an international Football Association. And rather in the same way that cricket deferred to the Marylebone Cricket Club, the English FA were approached to take the lead. When they failed to pick up the torch, Europe went ahead without them under the leadership of the Frenchman Robert Guerin. Once founded, the FA consented to become a member, but were later to pull out temporarily – a course of action that was to cost them a say in how the first World Cups were to be run. The blinkered attitude shown by the FA was not common to all Britons. Coaches like Jimmy Hogan, the man who was to help produce the famed Austrian 'Wunderteam' of the Thirties, laid the foundations for the continental style of football that even today contrasts strongly with the traditional English blood and thunder game. But England's first overseas tour seemed only to confirm the xenophobes' outlook, with four wins out of four against Austria (twice, 6-1 and 11-1), Hungary (7-0) and Bohemia (4-0). It would not be until 1929 that England would be defeated on foreign soil. By then, however, they would no longer be regarded as sole keepers of the football flame.

In Romania, the sport prospered under royal patronage – the Federation of Romanian Sports Societies was founded by Prince Carol who, as king would lead his team personally to the 1930 World Cup. Yugoslavia, too, had developed enough during the Twenties to compete there, and indeed reach the semi-finals as victors over Brazil. Developments were taking place even further afield. The United States, with its history of emigration from Britain and Ire-

PAGE 22: *Cardiff's Ferguson beats Arsenal goalkeeper Lewis to take the 1927 FA Cup.*

LEFT: *Artist Karl Hofer's 'Young Man*

with Football' of 1928.

BELOW LEFT: *An early Twenties postcard shows football thriving on the Continent. Note the lightweight*

sports shoes.

ABOVE: *This advertisement dates from 1890, and the football shows an abiding English influence.*

BELOW: *One of the first German soccer tournaments for young men was held in Berlin in February 1894.*

land, was clearly ripe for exploitation – and with the steel industry adopting the game, many footballers were tempted to cross the Atlantic in the Twenties and try their luck. The strength of South American teams like Argentina and Uruguay had been brought to European attention by the 1928 Olympic final, contested in Amster-

dam and won, as in the previous tournament, by Uruguay. Such events also acted as shop windows for such players as Raimondo Orsi, the spirited winger signed by Juventus, to settle in Spain or Italy – a migration that continued into the Eighties with players like the talented Maradona accepting the lure of the lira.

ABOVE: *Germany, in the striped shirts, lose 4-1 to Uruguay in the 1928 Olympic final, a result that emphasised South American strength.*

LEFT: *Another view of the same game. Staged in Amsterdam, it proved South American teams could compete in European conditions – the reverse was not always the case.*

POSTWAR PROGRESS

The First Division was extended by two clubs after World War I, with Arsenal and Chelsea taking the new places. But despite this shot in the arm for the South, the League Championship continued to be dominated by the North, aided in no small measure by Huddersfield's hat-trick in 1923-26. Only when Herbert Chapman moved his extensive skills to Arsenal did the South break the stranglehold.

Individual and collective goalscoring feats reached their zenith in the interwar years. George Camsell of Middlesbrough rewrote the goalscoring record books in 1926-27, notching 59 of the 122 goals that secured the Second Division title for his team. Less well known is his record number of hat-tricks: no fewer than nine. The end of the previous season, however, had seen him on the transfer list for the princely sum of £50, but there had been no takers. That his glut of goals followed the change of the offside law to tip the odds more in the attackers' favour was clearly no coincidence.

Everton's 102-goal total in 1927-28 was only the second time since 1893 that the magic 100-goal barrier had been broken in the top flight. If things were rosy for Everton at the top in 1928, then there was little to cheer at the foot of the table as the last nine teams were bracketed by just two points: Tottenham and Middlesbrough were relegated with 38 and 37 points respectively. Spurs thus established (and still hold) the unwanted distinction of having the largest points total of any club relegated from the top two divisions. Middlesbrough bounced back as champions in the following year. Sheffield Wednesday topped the League for two consecutive years, in 1928-29 with the lowest total (52 points) for a 42-match programme but extending their lead to 10 points the second time round. It was now by no means unusual, however, for clubs to break the three-figure goal barrier. In 1930-31, Arsenal (127), Aston Villa (128) and Sheffield Wednesday (102) all managed it.

Lower down the League, things had been changing at a rapid pace. A Third Division of 22 clubs had been established for a single season in 1920-21 before the League underwent its biggest expansion yet. Instead of one 22-club division spanning Crystal Palace (the winners, for the record) to Merthyr and Newport in the west it was deemed sensible to add a 20-club Third Division North,

bringing in clubs on the fringe. The Third Divisions North (20 clubs) and South (22) brought the strength to 86 clubs; by 1923-24 another couple had been added to bring all four divisions to 22 clubs apiece. The 1950-51 season saw the League expand to its present 92 clubs by adding an extra two clubs apiece to the lower divisions.

The two regional divisions fed one club apiece into the Second Division, but this could cause its own problems. The arbitrary division of the country into two sections could mean teams in the Midlands being obliged to switch to redress the balance depending on the location of promotion and relegation candidates, Walsall being one such 'makeweight'. This concept prevailed until 1957-58, when it was decided that regionalisation would be scrapped and the bottom halves of both tables amalgamated as the new Fourth Division, the remainder staying in the (plain) Third. As football lost its constituency in the Eighties, the idea of regionalisation and part-time football was once more to return to the agenda.

RIGHT: *George Camsell, whose record 59-goal haul in 1926-27 included nine hat-tricks. Camsell's feat was exceeded by 'Dixie' Dean in the following season, both assisted by the recently modified offside law.*

RIGHT: *Herbert Chapman (left, in suit) with his Huddersfield team in 1922. The Yorkshire side won three consecutive Championships later in the decade, as well as finishing runners-up twice and appearing in four Cup Finals.*

CHAPMAN'S CHAMPIONS

Highbury's marble halls are part of football legend; within them stands a bust of their most famous manager. Herbert Chapman was first of a breed – the star manager. Until his astute guidance took unfancied Huddersfield from nowhere to the dizzy heights of League champions for three years in a row, few supporters knew who managed anyone other than their own club. Huddersfield Town's was hardly the most glamorous of histories. Since forming in 1908 and rising from the Second Division in the first postwar season as runners-up, they had finished 17th and 14th. Yet under Chapman their form was a revelation. From 1922-23 onwards they achieved positions of 3rd, 1st and 1st, winning the Cup in 1922 as a curtain-raiser to their League ascendancy.

Chapman's earlier career had hardly shown such promise. After starting in management with Northampton Town in 1907, he had been banned with directors for involvement in illegal payments at Leeds City, a verdict later overturned. Joining Huddersfield as assistant in 1920, he ascended to the management seat within a month. He left in 1925 for the challenge of managing Arsenal – the major southern club with resources and aspirations to challenge the dominance of the North – following the dismissal of Leslie Knighton under whom they had slipped to 20th. Chairman Norris concluded his advertisement with the words, 'Anyone thinking of dispensing large sums of money on transfers need not apply.' This policy was soon forgotten as Arsenal became known as the 'Bank of England' club – but the return of Charles Buchan at 34, for example, after a spell with Sunderland, paid for itself with a 21-goal haul in his first season, despite the £100 per goal transfer fee suggested by Chapman.

ABOVE: *Arsenal players (from left) Roberts, Hapgood, Davidson, Crayston and Moss admire the bust of their late manager Herbert Chapman unveiled at Highbury in October 1936.*

BELOW: *Chapman (seated right) with his Arsenal team in 1927, on the threshold of greatness despite a 1-0 Cup Final reverse against Cardiff.*

BELOW: *Buchan leads Arsenal out for their 1928 FA Cup semi-final against Blackburn at Filbert Street, Leicester.*

RIGHT: *Buchan's return to Arsenal from Sunderland at 34 was a Chapman master stroke: the veteran captain's tactical awareness was exemplary.*

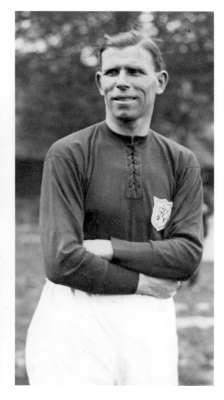

BELOW: *Arsenal stars Bob John and Cliff Bastin, selected to oppose each other in 1936's Wales-England international. The fact that half-back John was not a first-team regular emphasised Arsenal's strength in depth.*

Chapman's departure from Huddersfield coincided with the relaxation in the offside law, and Chapman was astute enough to turn this to advantage with his new club. Indeed, the move was born of necessity after a 7-0 drubbing at the hands of Newcastle in October 1925. At captain Buchan's suggestion, he withdrew the centre-half from his central midfield role in the 2-3-5 formation to plug the gap in front of the goalkeeper. The player initially filling this role was Jack Butler. The hole in midfield was filled by an inside-forward – the Scot Alex James, in this case – dropping back into a deep-lying position, feeding his winger with plenty of balls to chase. A measure of the tactic's success was the fact that speedy winger Cliff Bastin scored 33 goals from the wide position in season 1932-33 – a feat unlikely ever to be repeated in these days of wide men tackling back. Initially, the results were equally encouraging – the 0-7 reverse was followed by a 4-0 win at West Ham. The course of football tactics was to change as a result of these two fixtures.

The secret of Chapman's success was teamwork, fashioning a unit from talented individuals such as David Jack, James and Bastin that amounted to more than the sum of its constituent parts. Signed from Exeter at 17, Bastin at 21 had won every honour in the game – League, FA Cup and an England cap. The employment of James, who had been signed due to his great goalscoring record at Preston, in a feeder role could have rebounded on the manager, but it worked splendidly. Herbie Roberts, who succeeded Butler in the centre of the defence, was another risk: he had shown great attacking aggression as an old style centre-half. Now he was to become the most famous of these new stoppers, an imposing carrot-topped figure with the ability to win the ball in the air around who the defence was built. Full-backs Male and Hapgood pivoted on Roberts, providing cover should opposition forwards make a blind-side run. Alongside James and Bastin in the forward line stood Joe Hulme, Jack and wholehearted centre-forward Jack Lambert. Together they bamboozled Huddersfield – ironically their manager's former protégés – in the 1930 Cup Final, the 2-0 result not flattering them. Jack paralleled James's operations on the other flank, feeding winger Hulme to form the basis of the WM formation, so called because of the way the team looked when seen from above.

Chapman showed equal perspicacity in rebuilding his team to ensure continued success. The Cup-winning side of 1930 had only four members in common with that which had lost 1-0 to Cardiff three years before – and stood poised on the threshold of greatness. Their initial championship win in 1931 saw the trophy come to the capital for the first time – and with a record 66-point total at that. They were desperately unlucky to finish empty-handed the following season, running second to Everton in the League and losing 2-1 in the FA Cup final to Newcastle, a game decided by a disputed goal. But none of this worried Chapman: he continued the formula, and won the League again the following year.

The biggest shock in the Chapman era was the 2-0 third round defeat by Walsall in January 1933 – a reverse the country welcomed, as they do every Cup-fighting David who lays low a Goliath. With three internationals 'rested', another key player Hulme dropped and an abundance of that great leveller, mud, it was not to be their day. 'Lucky' Arsenal was a common and somewhat unfair taunt, but on that particular day the luck ran out. The championship, their second of the decade, was some consolation.

Chapman's untimely death in 1934 could not stop the Arsenal advance. In that same year, they supplied no fewer than seven of the England team that beat Italy. They won the League twice more in 1933-34 and 1934-35 under George Allison, equalling their former manager's record with Huddersfield 10 years before. A Cup win in 1936 and a fifth League Championship in 1937-38 established them as the team of the Thirties. Ted Drake led the forward line as the decade continued, and wrote himself into Highbury's record book on 14 December 1935. Aston Villa were the opposition, and all eyes at Villa Park were on new signing Alex Massie. Drake's first impact on the game was unimpressive, tripping as he strove to keep the ball in play and grazing himself on the cinder track surrounding the pitch. The crowd were amused, but Drake had the last laugh, completing a hat-trick in the first 19 minutes. Amazingly, he bettered the feat in the second half, three goals coming in a mere 12 minutes. Drake later notched his and Arsenal's seventh, wrapping up one of the best individual performances in League history. There were other notable names, too: left-back Eddie Hapgood, Wilf Copping, a combative defender whose habit of not shaving on match days added to his invincible aura, Tom Parker and George Maile, the latter later a backroom boy at Highbury. Yet in four Cup Finals, they employed four goalkeepers.

The final Arsenal haul makes impressive reading. Five championships and two Cup wins in nine seasons 1930-38. Add to that runners-up in both League and Cup, and you have the measure of a team that, until the arrival of Liverpool in the Seventies, stood unmatched. Little wonder Chapman himself continues to look down benevolently on Highbury's marble halls.

E. J. DRAKE

ABOVE: *Ted Drake, whose seven goals against Aston Villa in December 1935 remain an Arsenal milestone.*

BELOW: *Drake (right) swaps the red and white of Arsenal for an England shirt, menacing Italian goalkeeper Ceresoli on the Highbury turf in 1934.*

BELOW: *Arsenal avenged their FA Cup Final loss of 1927 by defeating Huddersfield 2-0 three years later. Here, Hulme, Seddon, Parker, Preedy and Bastin parade their prize around Wembley's perimeter.*

BOTTOM: *Ted Drake shows the dedication that made him a great goalscorer, lapping a frost-bound Highbury in late 1935.*

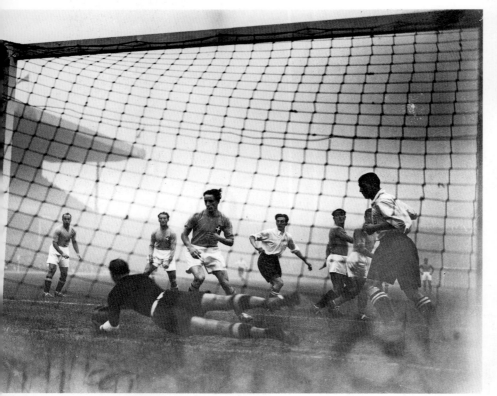

WEMBLEY! WEMBLEY!

Despite its unchallenged reputation as English soccer's most coveted trophy, the FA Cup had yet to find a permanent home. For the immediate three postwar seasons, the final was played at Stamford Bridge, Chelsea, before moving to a new stadium. When Wembley Stadium was built in 1922, the area surrounding it was far from urbanised. Its original use was for the unpopular British Empire Exhibition, for which a series of pavilions were built – but the stadium itself, completed in just 300 working days, was an unqualified success. The Football Association had been unusually far-sighted in displaying its interest, and as soon as its concrete terracing had been tested by an army regiment the gates were opened for the 1922-23 final. This, between Bolton Wanderers and West Ham, will forever be known as the 'White Horse Final' due to the intervention of mounted policeman PC George Scorey who forestalled a pitch invasion due to the uncontrollable crowd. Scorey was rewarded by complimentary tickets to subsequent finals, but never took these up: he was less than impressed with what he had seen. But finals have continued at Wembley to the present day, now with superior organisation and spectator facilities, save for the interruption of World War II.

That first-final problem had been caused partly by public curiosity about the new stadium and partly because of the participation of a London club. In any event, Huddersfield against Preston in 1922 had only attracted a 55,000 crowd. Official attendance on the day was 126,047 but contemporary reports almost double that. The match itself provided many stories, most amusing being the tale that a spectator provided the pass for Bolton's Ted Vizard to centre for John Smith's scoring volley. By this time, David Jack had become the first player to score at Wembley in a 2-0 win. The twin towers of Wembley somehow added lustre to the FA Cup legend, and Bolton were to take full advantage. They returned to

win twice more in the decade, in 1926 against Manchester City (1-0) and three years later against Portsmouth (2-0). Pym, Seddon, Nuttall and Butler, all England internationals, played in all three games along with Howarth.

ABOVE: *Mounted PC George Scorey in action at Wembley's first ever FA Cup Final – the 1923 fixture between Bolton and West Ham which attracted a crowd estimated at 250,000.*

BELOW: *A view from behind the goal at the same match. Although the playing area was eventually cleared, the crowds still lined the touchlines.*

Manchester City had gained an unwanted distinction in 1926 when they contrived to lose the Cup and be relegated from the First Division in the same season – the first finalists to do so. That their tenure on the top flight was lost with a missed penalty at Newcastle only added to their despair. In 1927, the Cup was taken out of England for the first (and so far only) time when Cardiff City beat Arsenal by a single goal, scored by centre-forward Ferguson. Just seven years later, however, Cardiff were having to undergo the in-dignity of applying for re-election to the League, with gates down below the 5000 mark. The 1929-30 season had seen Arsenal take their first major honour, the FA Cup, at a final that will

paradoxically be remembered as the 'Graf Zeppelin' final. The giant German airship flew over the stadium to witness a con-troversial first goal, a quickly taken free-kick worked between Alex James and winger Cliff Bastin as the Huddersfield players protested in vain. The Thirties were to see many more Cup legends made at Wembley.

BELOW: *Some of the estimated 120,000 spectators without tickets scale the walls of Wembley Stadium to see the first Cup Final there in 1923.*

RIGHT: *This 90-foot pipe was no deterrent to a would-be spectator attempting to gain entrance to the newly built Wembley Stadium. The crowd problems forced the authorities to look again at arrangements for such showpiece games.*

LEFT: *1927 saw the FA Cup leave England for the first (and only) time when Cardiff City beat Arsenal by a single goal. The victors are pictured in their Wembley dressing room.*

SCOTLAND

The English League has known dominance by individual teams, none perhaps more so than Liverpool in the Eighties. But never has it been dominated as completely as the Scottish League by Rangers and Celtic. Seventy-five league championship seasons lay between the first season of professionalism, 1893-94, and the creation of the Premier Division in the season 1974-75. Rangers claimed 34 of these and Celtic just six fewer, leaving just 13 opportunities for other teams to make their mark. The dominance of these two clubs has its base in religious rivalry rather than financial or footballing superiority, ensuring that they, of the six Glasgow clubs that once inhabited the top flight, should be and remain front-runners due to their fanatical support.

Celtic owed their foundation in 1887 to a Catholic monk, Brother Walfrid, his aim being to 'feed the needy children of the parishes of St Mary's and the Sacred Heart.' Rangers, in contrast, had grown from non-sectarian origins in 1873, being the creation of a group of oarsmen on the River Clyde. There is no record of any religious affiliation prior to their rival's appearance, yet despite this they were scrupulous in signing only Protestant players for over a century. In the same way as the talent drain south of the border impoverished Scottish football, so the Old Firm, as Rangers and Celtic became known, acted as a magnet for the Scottish talent that elected to remain in the country. With population statistics on the big city clubs' side – it is estimated that a circle drawn in a 50-mile radius of Glasgow encompasses over 70 per cent of Scottish population – gate receipts enabled the big two to buy anyone they wanted.

Their dominance was first challenged in the Twenties by Airdrie, who finished second for four consecutive seasons from 1922-23 without being able to overhaul Rangers (1923-25) and then Celtic. The Scottish Cup win in 1924, 2-0 against Hibernian, was some consolation and remains their major honour six decades on. In the late Twenties and early Thirties, Motherwell mounted a spirited challenge to Glasgow, bringing the championship back to lowly Fir Park in 1932. They secured the runners up position four time in seven surrounding seasons, losing to Celtic twice in the 1931 and 1933 Cup Finals. The goalscoring exploits of Bill McFadyen, who notched 52 in the championship season, were one of the cornerstones of their success.

But Celtic and Rangers marched on regardless. Rangers' 15 championships in the two interwar decades under the managership of William Struth, who took over for the 1920-21 season, are still revered by their fans. The team became household names – in one half of Glasgow, anyway – with left-winger Alan Morton the most famous of all. His supporting cast included Davie Meiklejohn (the captain) and Bob McPhail. Between the three of them, they won 30 championship and 13 Cup medals. The only club outside the First (now Premier) Division to win the Scottish Cup is East Fife, who managed the task in 1938 after five replays, one being the final. In truth, opponents Kilmarnock were only just hanging on to their top flight place, but Fife's achievement is none the less remarkable for that. The final was 1-1 and the replay ended two goals apiece, but two extra time goals saw the Methil side home. Hearts' John Harvey joined the club between the two games, receiving a winners medal for his first game. For all their dominance, Rangers were to suffer a

LEFT: *England goalkeeper Hufton is beaten by a shot from Scotsman Jackson during the 1928 Wembley international. Games between the 'auld enemies' have always attracted sellout crowds, as can clearly be seen here.*

quarter-century of SFA Cup failure, an inexplicable run which ended with a 4-0 defeat of the 'Auld Enemy' in 1928.

Internationals, especially with England, remained a cornerstone of the Scottish game – and one in 1928 will never be forgotten. A 5-1 scoreline ensured the 'Wembley Wizards' immortality in the annals of Scottish football. Right-winger Alex Jackson and inside-left Alex James split the spoils in conditions which clearly favoured them. With a forward line in which no-one exceeded five foot seven inches, the surprise was Jackson's hat-trick of headers. The Scottish League had continued through World War I, but the outbreak of hostilities in 1939 saw the usual fixtures curtailed. A series of regional leagues and cups was substituted.

As in England, the immediate postwar period saw interest in the game reach new heights, and with crowds at record levels the stage was set for another challenge to Glasgow domination despite Rangers achieving the first ever treble (League, Scottish Cup and League Cup) in 1949. The two Edinburgh teams were particularly well placed to mount this, with crowds often in excess of 30,000. Hibernian were first to show with championship wins in 1948, 1951 and 1952, running up in 1950 and 1953. Their chief goalscorer was inside-left Lawrie Reilly, with Eddie Turnbull a steadying captain and a future Scottish national manager, Willie Ormond, on the wing. Hearts recorded their first championship of the twentieth century in the season 1957-58, when they established a club record

points total of 62 and an astounding 132 goals, repeating the championship if not those totals two years later. The mainstay of their team was bustling midfielder Dave Mackay, soon to be spirited south to propel Tottenham to even greater glory.

Aberdeen won the League for the first time in their history in 1955, with Harry Yorston – son of 1930 record scorer Benny Yorston – appropriately among the goals. The previous season saw Pittodrie establish its all-time attendance record of 45,061 in a cup game against Hearts, proof of the great interest in Scottish football. The Scottish Cup, too, saw a plethora of unusual names inscribed upon it, with Motherwell (1952), Clyde (1955 and 1958), Falkirk (1957) and St Mirren (1959) all getting their hands on the silverware.

The honours share out fizzled out in the early Sixties, with the abolition of the maximum wage only hastening the talent drain to England and Glasgow alike. Highlights of this period were Dunfermline winning the Cup in 1961 when a lowly twelfth in the First Division and Dundee taking the championship a year later, with Alan Gilzean (later of Spurs) and Ian Ure (en route to Arsenal) prominent. The Dundee team entered the following season's European Cup more in hope than expectation, yet produced a major surprise when they hit Cologne for an 8-1 aggregate victory on their way to a semi-final place. This set the scene for a return to the Old Firm dominance which was only to be challenged in the Eighties – a challenge that was to bring many surprises in its wake.

LEFT: *The Aberdeen team relax on the eve of their title-clinching game in 1955. Crowds of up to 45,000 were not uncommon in their championship-winning season.*

RIGHT: *1955 saw Aberdeen win their first League title. Running out at Hearts' Tynecastle ground are Young, Martin, top scorer Yorston and Smith.*

'DIXIE'

If Scotland's major problem was the insidious drain of talent southwards across the border to England, Sunderland were one early First Division force to benefit, while their northeastern rivals Newcastle beat all when, in October 1928, they faced Leeds United with 10 Scots in their team. 1927-28 saw champions Everton notch a 102-goal total, the highest since 1920. One man was chiefly responsible – William Ralph 'Dixie' Dean, an unassuming centre-forward whose 60 goals beat the year-old record of Middlesbrough's Camsell by a single strike. When the final match of the season against Arsenal started he stood two behind, but a hat-trick drew the game 3-3 and took him to the record. Even more remarkable was the fact that Dean had played only 39 of Everton's 42 games that year. His previous season's form had been rather less remarkable, with 21 League goals to his credit – reasonable, however, for a striker whose team managed just 64 in total and who escaped relegation by a single place. His record-breaking season included 22 goals in Cup, international, international trial and inter-League games.

Everton in 1931 found all five forwards – Stein, Dean, Dunn, Critchley and Johnson – on the scoresheet at the Valley against Charlton Athletic – in the space of 18 minutes! The Second Division game finished 7-0 in favour of the eventual divisional champions. They had been relegated the previous season, just two years after winning the First Division championship. Their return to the top flight saw them collect the League and Cup in successive seasons – all of which must have been mystifying for their supporters.

Dean himself could thank his speed and exceptional heading ability for his goals, assisted of course by a change in the offside rule that gave him one less man to beat on his route to goal. Teammate Joe Mercer said of his speed off the mark, 'He had the ability to stand still until they went for him – and then he wasn't there.' Dean detested his nickname, apparently due to his black (supposedly Negroid) hair, and insisted on being known as Bill. He notched another important goal in the 3-0 1933 Cup Final win against Manchester City.

Dixie Dean wasn't alone in setting scoring records, although most of his rivals set them on a single match basis. Ted Drake of Arsenal's seven against Aston Villa in 1935 are detailed elsewhere, while Luton's Joe Payne went even better with 10 goals in a League match in 1934. Dean's replacement was Tommy Lawton, in many people's eyes Dean's rival as the best centre-forward Britain ever produced. Everton bought him from Burnley as a 17-year-old for £6500 in 1936, and he scored 34 goals to help them take the championship in 1938-39, the season he won the first of 23 England caps.

War took its toll of his competitive career, and moves to Chelsea (1945) and, surprisingly, Third Division Notts County (1947, for a record £20,000) presaged moves to Brentford and Arsenal. Lawton was one of English football's most travelled players, and one of the most talented.

The immediate prewar years saw an attendance boom in League football. On 23 February 1935, no fewer than 77,582 paying customers saw Manchester City play the eventual champions, Arsenal. This figure which amazingly does not include season ticket holders brought the official attendance to Maine Road's nominal capacity of 80,000. Now, of course, safety standards and improved amenities give the ground a capacity of half that. The story wasn't as rosy everywhere, however, with clubs going to the wall in increasing numbers. And where the game could have given comfort to those hardest hit by the Depression, it was obvious that some communities, in Wales, for example, were no longer able to support a Football League team. Aberdare Athletic were voted out in favour of Torquay in 1927, Merthyr Town for Thames in 1930. Thankfully for the Principality, Newport's exile in 1931 only lasted a season.

The Northeast, too, suffered with club closures. Durham City went in 1928, Ashington in 1929 and South Shields moved to more prosperous Gateshead the following year. In the Northwest, Stalybridge Celtic (1923), Nelson (1931) and Wigan Borough all fell. Wigan resigned from the League in the middle of a season, setting an unhappy precedent only matched once since by Accrington (in 1961-62). While the big-city clubs continued regardless, the grassroots of English League football were to remain starved of cash until the postwar boom brought a brief period of prosperity to the League's lower divisions.

If Arsenal were the team of the Thirties, then Wolves had every right to consider that theirs, but for war, would have been the team of the Forties. Created by Major Frank Buckley, the Midlands team were just hitting their stride in those fateful prewar years; fifth in 1937, second in 1938 and 1939, and reaching the FA Cup Final as hot favourites with a 19-3 goal tally only to crash 4-1 to Portsmouth. The major had a penchant for publicity, provoking a FA enquiry with his players supposedly injected with monkey glands to improve their game. More concretely, he had a new gymnasium built and ruled his young players – mostly cast-offs from other clubs – with a rod of iron. As it turned out, the war left Wolves the maybe team, and Buckley the nearly man. He left the club in 1944 after a boardroom reshuffle. Stan Cullis, his captain, was to succeed him eventually and find a good measure of postwar success.

LEFT: *William Ralph 'Dixie' Dean of Everton, one of the legendary figures of English football, whose 60-goal record haul in the 1927-28 season helped Everton to a 102-goal total.*

FORWARD WITH FIFA

Although it was only to come into its own in the postwar years, the World Cup was in fact inaugurated in 1928 by the World Congress, a gathering convened by FIFA. They decided that the national teams should play every four years for the privilege of being acclaimed the world's best. The first of these tournaments was held in Uruguay. The venue was significant in two other respects: the competition's final stages were broadly to alternate between Europe and South America, while for the first two World Cups, at least, the home country emerged victorious. The Cup the teams played for was known as the Jules Rimet trophy, named after the Honorary President of FIFA from 1921 to 1954. Standing a mere 2ft 3in in height, the solid gold statuette designed by French sculptor Abel Lafleur weighed 12lb 3 ozs. The competition had first been mooted in 1904, the year FIFA initially convened in Paris without British representation, and took shape in 1924 when the Paris Olympics saw Uruguay's amateur team impress the world while picking up the gold medal. It was this that persuaded FIFA Secretary Henri Delaunay to declare in 1926 that 'international football can no longer be held within the confines of the Olympics, and many countries where professionalism is now recognised and organised cannot any longer be represented by their best players.'

Uruguay retained the Olympic title in 1928 and, by virtue of offering to pay travel and hotel expenses for the contestants, persuaded aspiring hosts Italy, Holland, Spain and Sweden to withdraw their bids. Despite this subsidy, the host country still proved successful in turning a profit. None of the four disappointed would-be hosts competed, a three-week boat trip perhaps proving the sticking point. Thus it was that just 13 nations – and only four from Europe – took part in the first World Cup championship, obviating the need for a qualifying competition. British national teams were not involved, and it was to be 20 years before they deigned to take part – an example of the blinkered view of the game's governing body, the Football Association.

The promised Centenary Stadium, celebrating 100 years of Uruguayan independence had, predictably, not been finished. The same could also be said for the game between Argentina and France which the referee brought to a close six minutes early, denying the French an equalising goal. The referee was Brazilian, a fact that raised questions of continental bias that crop up perenially to this day (though most often voiced by South Americans). Whether true or not, it remained a fact that the Cup has only once been won by team from a continent other than that in which the tournament was held (Brazil in 1958). Thus the presence of Argentina in the 1930 final to face the hosts, by now playing in the finally complete Centenary Stadium, ran true to form. Both teams had romped their semi-finals 6-1, Argentina over the United States and their six former British professionals, and Brazil over Yugoslavia.

With Argentina and Uruguay near neighbours, the final was played in a predictably fanatical atmosphere. Ten packet boats had been chartered to take Argentinian fans across the River Plate, and their support certainly lent the event an edge. The teams, too, took things to extremes: each wanted a ball of their own manufacture. But though Argentina won the toss in that case, it was almost all that went right for them. After conceding an early goal to Dorado, they equalised through Peucelle and took the lead with a disputed strike from the outstanding Stabile. After half-time, however, the tide flowed the other way and Uruguayan goals by Cea, Irarte and Castro decided the issue.

Of the four European contenders, Yugoslavia had fared best by reaching the semi-final. The United States' semi-final appearance had justified their seeding along with Uruguay, Argentina and Brazil. The other Europeans were Romania, France and Belgium. So it was that the first World Cup victory was celebrated in Montevideo with a national holiday declared, ships' sirens blaring and flags and banners waving. In Buenos Aires, however, it was a different story with the unfortunate stoning of the Uruguayan Embassy being halted only through police opening fire to disperse the crowds. It was to be 20 years before the World Cup tournament – and the trophy itself – returned to South America.

LEFT: *Jules Rimet presents the World Cup trophy that bore his name to the first winners, Uruguay, in the shape of that country's FA President Dr Paul Jude in 1930.*

PLAYING THE GAME (2)

As mentioned elsewhere, Herbert Chapman was quick to profit from the 1925 change in the offside law, an event that neatly divided his managership of Huddersfield and Arsenal. With the less restrictive offside law now operative, the two-man defensive line was looking even more vulnerable, despite the half-backs' reinforcement – and with the centre-half playing a roving role there was little to prevent opponents taking advantage of the yawning space down the middle to press home their attacks in the most direct way possible. Chapman plugged the gap by inventing the stopper centre-half, simultaneously converting the inside-forwards to deeper-lying linkmen between defence and attack. The wing-halves continued their ball-winning role, feeding the inside-forwards who in turn would put their wingers away.

The new three-man defence operated thus: the full-backs would pivot round the centre-half (often himself termed the 'pivot'), reacting to the man in possession. The full-back farthest from the ball would cover behind for blind-side runs. The half-backs would pivot in similar fashion. This was known as the WM formation, the stylised shape the players made when viewed from above. When numerical designations became the vogue, the description was 3-4-3: three at the back, four in midfield (assuming both inside-forwards dropped back to play as linkmen in the centre-half's stead) and three forwards, the two wingers and the centre-forward.

In Britain, it was usual to settle for a tactic and stick to it. The third-back game was to rule unchallenged for nearly 30 years. Europe, however, was far more amenable to experiment – and ironically it was British coaches like Arthur Rowe (ex-Spurs) and Jimmy Hogan (ex-Fulham) who led the way, practising the coach's art in Hungary and Austria respectively. It was no coincidence that Austria's 'Wunderteam' were the acclaimed footballing force of the Thirties, while Hungary were the team to reveal English complacency so cruelly in 1953.

Although not compulsory until 1939, team numbering was allowed in 1933, adding spice to the tactics game. The numbers used in the first match, the FA Cup Final between Everton and Manchester City were from 1 to 22, ensuring each player had an individual number. But this was soon amended to a system that started at the goalkeeper (Number 1), through right and left-backs (2,3), the half-back line – right (4), centre (5) and left (6) – to the right wing (7), inside-right (8), centre-forward (9), inside and ouside-left (10, 11). The recognition factor made it easier for the hard-pressed referee to administer punishment to offenders, and also assisted players in keeping tabs on the right man. It wasn't long, however, before the simple expedient of shuffling players around, giving them numbers at variance with their true positions, gave rise to a certain amount of confusion. Some continental countries' numbering systems gave the centre-back the Number 3 shirt, indicating his position at the centre of the back line.

The corner kick had been an early addition to the rules of the game, but it had enjoyed only the status of an indirect free-kick. The Scottish Football Association proposed in 1924 that a goal should be able to be scored direct by the kicker – but an incident when Everton winger Sam Chedgzoy dribbled a corner into the Tottenham net in 1925 caused the FA to add a new rider to the rule: 'The kicker shall not play the ball a second time until it has been touched by another player.'

LEFT: *Herbert Chapman (left) introduced the stopper centre-half to the English game, thus forming a three-man defensive line that, together with the change in the offside law in 1925, was the major tactical change of the Twenties.*

WORLD CUPS 1934/38

The 1934 World Cup was held in Italy, thereby giving European teams their turn at 'home advantage'. It was not, however, for this reason that the defending champions, Uruguay, set a precedent by being the first – and so far – only country not to defend their title. Italy were actually obliged to qualify: both holders and hosts have always since been excused the chore. But in Uruguay's case, a player strike prevented them from giving the competition adequate preparation and was the apparent reason for their non-appearance. No such worries for the home team, under the benevolent eye of dictator Benito Mussolini and, officially, team manager Vittorio Pozzo. Most people expected them to win through to the final where their logical opponents would be Austria, the 'Wunderteam' of manager Hugo Meisl and English coach Jimmy Hogan which had inflicted an embarrassing 4-2 reverse on the Italians in Turin a mere matter of months before.

The Austrians built their game on short passing and great ball control – almost a throwback to the classic Scottish game. Ironic, then, that they should have beaten Scotland 5-0 in May 1931 as they began their World Cup warm-up, remaining unbeaten for 10 matches thereafter. Germany (6-0, then 5-0), Switzerland (8-1) and Hungary (8-2) all went under the cosh before England inflicted a 4-3 defeat at Stamford Bridge in 1932. No wonder they were feared.

Whereas Uruguay's World Cup had been organised on a four-group pool or league format to determine the semi-finalists, Italy decided upon a straight knockout for the 16 teams involved. This seemed rough justice for the South Americans, who had little time to acclimatise – and so it proved. 1930's beaten finalists Argentina (with a totally rebuilt team) and neighbours Brazil both fell at the first hurdle, having ludicrously crossed the world to play 90 minutes apiece. Mexico did likewise to lose to the United States in a qualifying eliminator; the US team survived only to lose 7-1 to their hosts. The extent of the qualifying tournament confirmed that the

World Cup was indeed a going concern: the 32 entrants included eight from South America and one apiece from Asia and Africa. Despite the preponderance of European sides, none of the British countries competed.

Italy stumbled in the second round, only drawing with unfancied Spain in a game so rough that Pizziolo broke a leg and the Spaniards had to make seven changes forced by injury for the replay. Italy triumphed by a single goal, while the 'derby' between Austria and Hungary was so ill-tempered that the latter's Markos was sent off. 2-1 victors Austria met the host country in the semi-finals and not in the final, as neutrals had hoped.

Both semi-final games were all-European affairs. In the first, the weather favoured the more physical Italy, a downpour making a quagmire of the Milan pitch. A single goal by the Argentinian Guaita was all that separated the teams, with Austria's star Zischek spurning a last-gasp chance to equalise, a goal-kick having cut out the churned-up midfield to land at his feet. The second semi-final between Czechoslovakia and Germany was a restrained affair by contrast, the Czechs rallying to win 3-1 after two-goal striker Nejedly's opener had been equalised from long range by Noack. The respected Czech goalkeeper Planicka had been at fault for failing to pick up the shot – and it was a second mistake by him, this time in the final, that let Italy come back apparently from the dead to salvage their World Cup hopes.

Played in front of a less than capacity Rome crowd, the game had amazingly lacked passion – and when the Czech winger Puc struck

BELOW: *The Italian team that profited from home advantage by winning the second World Cup in 1934. Their final opponents were Czechoslovakia.*

after an hour it seemed as if an upset was on the cards. But when Italy's second Argentine-born winger, Orsi, swirled a tricky shot into the corner of the net just eight minutes from time, the stage was set for a revival. Certainly it would have been harsh to pin all the blame on Planicka: after all, when Orsi tried to recreate his shot for photographers the following day without a goalkeeper, he failed in a score of attempts. Meanwhile, extra time was being played, and centre-forward Schiavio, who hitherto had had an unexceptional game, drew on what he later called 'the strength of desperation' to hit the winner. The final will provide a footnote in World Cup history as being the only one where both teams were captained by their respective goalkeepers.

Italy had won, then, and home advantage had told. It was fortunate for them that they would not be called upon to defend their trophy in South America's inhospitable climes: the decision to prefer France to Argentina as the venue for 1938 was made at FIFA's 1936 congress and, predictably perhaps, led to Argentina refusing to participate. This in turn led to a riot in Buenos Aires. Uruguay maintained their policy of non-participation – but their absence was to a small extent compensated for by exotic new names. The Dutch East Indies, Cuba (last minute replacements for Mexico) and, for the first time, Poland were among the record 36 entrants to make it to the final stages.

Once more, the competition finals were run on an exclusively knockout basis. Italy could easily have provided the shock of the tournament, all but departing at the first hurdle. They overcame the Norwegians 2-1 only in extra time and with the help of a goal against them in normal play disallowed . The game of the tournament, however, was a Europe versus South America clash between Brazil and World Cup debutants Poland. Brazil scraped through 6-5 with the benefit of extra time, having trailed 3-1 at the interval. Conditions hardly favoured them: indeed, centre-forward Leonidas attempted to play the second half without boots so wet was the pitch, but the referee made him put them back on. Booted or not, he contributed four goals to the spectacle, as did Willimowski the Polish inside-left. The Brazilian effort was even more praiseworthy in that the team contained six new internationals. Germany also fielded three debutants from Austria; that country having been annexed by the Fatherland, they were now 'eligible'. They exited, unlamented, 4-2 after a replay at the hands of Switzerland. The unfancied horses, meanwhile, enjoyed mixed fortunes. Cuba beat powerful Romania 2-1 after a 3-3 draw, while the Dutch East Indies conceded six Hungarian goals without reply.

The major match of the second round was hosts versus holders in Paris. A brace of opening goals, one for each side, was followed by periods of stalemate before the match was settled in Italy's favour by Piola's double strike. Elsewhere Sweden ended the Cuban dream emphatically by an 8-0 margin. But the game between those two most skilful of teams, Brazil and Czechoslovakia, made headlines for all the wrong reasons. Goalkeeper Planicka sustained a broken arm, goalscorer supreme Nejedly a fractured leg. Three lesser but still serious injuries and three sendings off – two Brazilians, one Czech – completed an ugly picture. The result, all but academic, was a 1-1 draw, with Brazil winning 2-1 in a thankfully unremarkable replay featuring no less than 15 team changes from the two sides.

ABOVE AND LEFT: *The meeting of Italy and Hungary in the 1938 World Cup final pitted the physical against the purists – and Italy's all-action style saw them triumph by 4-2 to retain the Cup.*

Brazil were not to survive for long, however, falling 2-1 to Italy in Marseilles. The second semi-final at Colombes, was rather more one-sided, Sweden's 35-second opener from Nyberg being answered no less than five times by the magnificent Magyars. It set the scene for a dramatic and entertaining final. Top scorer of the tournament was Brazil's Leonidas with eight, including two in the 4-2 third-place win against Sweden. He had been absent, 'rested', for the semi against Italy – a decision the Brazilians must have re-

gretted given the closeness of the scoreline.

The final saw Italy's physical bustle and energy overcome Hungary's skilful yet static football by 4 to 2, flying winger Colaussi and veteran striker Piola splitting the spoils. After four years as champions Italy had retained the Cup – and, though no-one could have known at the time, would retain it for a further 12.

RIGHT AND BELOW: *Italy acclaim their victory – a win that was to see them retain the World Cup until the first postwar tournament in 1950.*

PART III

Europe
and Beyond

1945-65

POSTWAR DEVELOPMENTS

The war years of 1939-45 saw football in Britain continue on a makeshift regional basis. When war broke out, the season had barely started, with no club having fulfilled more than three fixtures. Tragically, of course, so many players lost the best seven years of their careers, and many – for reasons of age, injury or death – would be seen no more. Among those who fell were Harry Goslin (Bolton), Herbie Roberts (Arsenal) and Albert Clarke (Blackburn Rovers). Moscow Dynamo's late-1945 tour of Britain rekindled the country's appetite for football. The first game of the tour was at London's Stamford Bridge, home to Chelsea FC – and demand for tickets was unprecedented. Estimates of the eventual gate were around the 100,000 mark – the highest attendance figure ever recorded at an English club ground – and this was merely a friendly. For the record, the match ended a 3-3 draw.

As the League programme restarted, the country took stock. Although the four divisions stood as they had before hostilities commenced, many teams were recognisable in name only. What, for instance, would the future hold for Wolves? They had seemed likely to become the team of the Forties, having ended the Thirties with two runners-up positions and a Cup Final appearance under Major Buckley. They were rebuilding, while other clubs shuffled as many as 42 men (Hull City's unenviable record) in an attempt to find the right postwar blend. To complicate matters further, the infamous 'Big Freeze' extended the season into mid-June. Nevertheless, the British public returned to football in their thousands, with demobilisation money to spend and unaccustomed leisure time in which to enjoy it. It didn't seem to matter who they went to watch: Third Division attendances of 25,000 were not unusual in a season in which 35,000,000 paying customers flocked through the turnstiles to watch League football. Five million more saw the following season's fare. The 1948-49 season was even better attended, and the aggregate figure of 41,271,424 registered that year has never been surpassed.

So which clubs were making the headlines in front of such large crowds? Liverpool emerged victors from the first postwar First Division fixtures, Arsenal winning the following year and Portsmouth were champions in 1949 and 1950 – the latter's only such honours ever. Manchester United were pipped at the post for the first three seasons, gaining some recompense through their 1948 Cup win. 1950 saw the League expand from 88 clubs to the present 92: Colchester, Scunthorpe, Shrewsbury and Gillingham the happy entrants. Scunthorpe triumphed over Workington and Wigan, who had initially tied for membership of the Third Division North (two clubs being admitted into each). Instead of a two-horse race, the remaining place was re-advertised and Scunthorpe made it. Workington replaced New Brighton the following year, but Wigan took another three decades to make it.

PAGE 42: *Pictured in the colours of Arsenal, George Eastham made soccer history by challenging the 'retain and transfer' system prevalent in British football, his victory paving the way for players to become free agents once out of contract.*

BELOW: *Moscow Dynamo players line up before the kick-off of their late-1945 tour game against Chelsea. A crowd of around 100,000 watched this 3-3 friendly.*

RIGHT: *The Soviet goalkeeper Khomich tips a Chelsea centre over the crossbar.*

BELOW: *Moscow Dynamo take the field at Stamford Bridge. Their brief tour predated organised competitive European football by over a decade.*

England were limbering up for their first World Cup, a 10-0 victory in Portugal in May 1947 making the world sit up and take notice. Stan Mortensen and Tom Lawton were the stars that day with four goals apiece. England had two world-class players in Tom Finney and the legendary Stanley Matthews, but both were right-wingers. Switching Finney to the left failed to blunt his goalscoring instincts: he and Matthews scored one apiece. Finney's goal was England's fourth goal, a magical solo effort just before half-time in which he beat three men and then the goalkeeper from an acute angle after receiving the ball on the half-way line.

The same forward line of Matthews, Mortensen, Lawton, Mannion and Finney took on the Italians in Turin exactly one year later, this time scoring four without reply. This, if anything, was an even more impressive victory over a side including seven of the great Torino team that ran away with four Italian championships before being cruelly decimated in a 1949 plane crash. Goals from Mortensen, Lawton and a brace from Finney settled the issue, with goalkeeper Frank Swift performing minor miracles at the other end. As the World Cup just two years later was to prove, England flattered in this case to deceive, but it was fitting that in an atmosphere of postwar revival the national team's fortunes should mirror those of the domestic game.

LEFT: *The inimitable Stanley Matthews, seen here in the stripes of his hometown club Stoke.*

BELOW: *Matthews in the colours of Blackpool with which he was to gain a Cup Winners' medal at the age of 38.*

WORLD CUP 1950

The year 1950 marked a turning point in British football as the first time the World Cup was to be contested with British national teams among the entrants. Qualification was to be a result of the Home International Championship, the first and second-placed teams being eligible for the finals in Brazil. England won and duly took up their allotted place, but Scotland declined the invitation despite claiming the second slot. As it transpired, England's unfortunate experience probably confirmed the Scots' decision. Yet they travelled in expectation of at least a medal, being ante-post favourites alongside Brazil thanks to their record of 22 wins and 2 draws in 28 postwar internationals. These had included the famous 10-0 thrashing of Portugal. Furthermore they now had a full-time manager in Walter Winterbottom, but he still had to report to a selection committee.

Playing their first match at the brand-new Rio Stadium and beating Chile by a 2-0 margin, they travelled to Belo Horizonte for what seemed the formality of dispatching the United States. England's downfall was plotted by one Eddie McIlvenny, a free transfer man who'd last graced the Football League with Third Division Wrexham. The 1-0 defeat, by a goal from Gaetjens, was the greatest humiliation ever suffered by the English national team. When the side lost to Spain by a similar score, albeit after having a legitimate goal disallowed for offside, it was plain their interest in the Cup was over. Embarrassingly, a 'second rank' Football Association XI had earlier beat the US World Cup team on their home turf.

Like Uruguay 20 years previously, the Brazilian pledge to build a new stadium for the event failed to match the timetable required. The 200,000-seater Maracana was finished for the final with the aid of the armed forces, but had to be used in its uncompleted state for the earlier matches. Argentina, like Scotland, were absentees of their own choosing, having had a disagreement with their neighbours. Others to stay away included Czechoslovakia, still recovering from the ravages of war, France (who declined to play in the group in which they were drawn due to the 2000-mile distance between venues), Portugal, Hungary, Russia and Austria. Germany was at this time excluded from FIFA membership.

The result of all this was a badly organised and poorly attended tournament that gave Brazil the advantage of playing all but one of their six matches in Rio. The gruelling cross-country travel that had deterred France was all too common, with unbalanced pools meaning that Uruguay had only to beat Bolivia (they managed this small matter 8-0) to qualify for the final group. FIFA Secretary Henri Delaunay had resigned from the World Cup committee on a point of principle, disagreeing with the decision that pools (leagues) should replace the straight knockout system used since 1934.

Holders Italy were not among the absentees, although the previous year's air crash that decimated the Torino team had a devastating effect: eight of the national side lost their lives. Many players opted for a gruelling sea journey, understandable but in the circumstances hardly suitable preparation, while the resignation of team manager Pozzo over tactics had not helped, his duties being assumed by a two-man committee. Brazil as hosts had to be among the favourites. The two teams' fortunes contrasted strongly: Brazil beat Mexico 4-0 at a rubble-strewn Maracana without breaking sweat, while Italy's 3-2 defeat by unfancied Sweden was to prove fatal.

The fact that the pool system was retained for the final stages of the tournament theoretically deprived the spectators of a Cup Final to cheer. Nevertheless, the fixture list contrived to throw up the next best thing, a match between the top two contenders with the winner assured of the Cup. Neutral money was on the home team, which had allowed opponents Sweden and Spain a token goal apiece before despatching them for six and seven. A draw against Uruguay was all that was needed to ensure the most popular of results and a bonus of £10,000 per player, but they failed at the last gasp, thanks to an heroic display by Uruguayan guardian Maspoli.

The Uruguayans were prepared to play a containing game in the face of pressure from Brazil and their supporters. But a goal from Friaça two minutes after half-time forced a change of tactics, and Schiaffino and Ghiggia profited from confusion on Brazil's left flank to rake in the goals that brought the World Cup back to South America – and Uruguay – after 20 years of exile.

RIGHT: *England's first team manager Walter Winterbottom. A respected coach, Winterbottom worked in tandem with a selection committee. Not until Alf Ramsey succeeded him did an England manager have the final say in team selection.*

THE MATTHEWS FINAL

Blackpool, a small seaside town in Lancashire, provided the archetypal FA Cup heroes. Before the abolition of the maximum wage saw the glamour clubs monopolise talent, and before Manchester United and the burgeoning motorway network siphoned off home-town support, Blackpool enjoyed their moments of glory. Their record of three finals in five years, losing in 1948 and 1951, was not perhaps exceptional. But it was for the 1953 game, which will forever be dubbed the 'Matthews Final', that they will go down in football history. Defeats at the hands of Manchester United and Newcastle had given the team valuable experience. But no player on the pitch could boast more experience than Stanley Matthews, then a veteran of 38 years. No-one could have foreseen that he would later return to his home-town club of Stoke City – his only other League club – and take them back into the First Division at the age of 50.

In 1953, however, it was amazing enough that a man in early middle age could take up a wide position in which speed usually played so great a part. Matthews, of course, had other attributes. He also shared the tangerine shirt with several useful players like centre-forward Stan Mortensen. Bolton had Nat Lofthouse, the Lion of Vienna, whose opening goal secured him the distinction of having scored in every round. Despite a Mortensen equaliser, goals by Moir and a hobbling Bell had given Bolton a seemingly unassailable 3-1 lead before fate – and Matthews – took a hand.

Bolton's left-back Banks was suffering from cramp, while their left half-back Bell sustained an early injury and played out time almost as a makeshift winger. Matthews, far from makeshift himself, centred for Bolton keeper Handson to fumble and Mortensen to add Blackpool's second on 68 minutes. The same player scored direct from a free kick after 89 minutes. Matthews then came into his own, defying expectations that the lush Wembley turf would take a toll of his stamina by demonstrating consummate ball artistry to set up Bill Perry's injury-time winner with a typical cross.

Though Blackpool's win is still fondly remembered, Newcastle

ABOVE: *Stanley Matthews, one of the greatest players the English game ever produced. His performance for Blackpool in the 1953 FA Cup Final has passed into legend.*

LEFT: *A scramble in the Bolton goalmouth is cleared by keeper Handson. The custodian was, however, at fault with Blackpool's second goal.*

were certainly the Cup team of the Fifties. Their hero was Jackie Milburn, whose shrewd timing brought him many goals from deep. George Robledo, born in Chile but adopted by Tyneside, was his striking partner, and both set up wins in 1951 and 1952. The first win was secured by a brace of Milburn goals, while a single Robledo effort was enough to dispose of Arsenal. This second win was the first time a team had retained the Cup since Blackburn's hat-trick in the 1884-86 seasons.

The postwar Cup threw up its share of giantkillers. Yeovil Town, led by future manager of QPR and Fulham Alec Stock, beat mighty Sunderland on their treacherously sloping pitch in the 1948-49 Third Round, only to be thrashed 8-0 by Manchester Utd for their pains. United had beaten Blackpool 4-2 the previous year to take the Cup, the first silverware to adorn their boardroom since the arrival of Matt Busby as manager. But United's is another story.

BELOW LEFT: Newcastle captain (and later manager) Joe Harvey cradles the FA Cup after the first of their Wembley wins in 1951.

BOTTOM: Newcastle keeper Fairbrother saves from Blackpool's Slater in the 1951 Final. He kept a clean sheet as the Tynesiders won 2-0.

BELOW: Chilean-born George Robledo, in Newcastle's stripes, is thwarted by Blackpool's Farm. His striking partner Jackie Milburn scored both match-winning goals.

THE MIGHTY MAGYARS

The Hungarian football team of the Fifties will forever be remembered as one of the greatest national sides ever seen. Consider their record: between a 7-2 defeat by Sweden in 1943 and a 4-2 reverse against Czechoslovakia in 1956 they were unbeaten on their own soil, while a four-year period in the Fifties saw them complete a 29-game sequence of home and away games without defeat. Predictably for a country which has yet to win a World Cup, that run was destined to end in a World Cup Final against West Germany in 1954.

Their postwar exile behind the Iron Curtain ended in 1952 when they participated in – and won in convincing fashion – the Olympic title in Helsinki. Built around the midfield general and captain Ferenc Puskas ('The Galloping Major' to the British press) and his educated left foot, the team had other stars too. Sandor 'Golden Head' Kocsis possessed enviable ability in the air for his height; Nandor Hidegkuti played as a deep-lying centre-forward, switching back and forth with Puskas and Kocsis to score with a venomous right foot; and Josef Bozsic, the engine room of the team driving them forward from the right-half position. Less celebrated but certainly no less important were wide men Zoltan Czibor and Budai II. Meanwhile, goalkeeper Gyula Grosics pioneered the tactic so widely seen in the Eighties of leaving his goal area to operate almost as an extra outfield player. Coach of the team was Gyula Mandi, operating under the Deputy Minister of Sport Gustav Sebes.

Born in 1926, captain Puskas had grown up in both the physical and footballing senses in the tough streets of Budapest. He joined his local club Kispest, but was later to join the army club Honved under a system where they could 'draft' the country's best players. His debut game for his country against Austria at the age of 18 saw him notch his first goal – a goal-a-game record he was to maintain with apparent ease, scoring 85 times in 84 appearances.

Undoubtedly the best-publicised Hungarian win – in Britain, at least – was the 6-3 drubbing of England at Wembley in November 1953. Amazingly, this was England's first ever home defeat by a 'foreign' side and, unlike the 'fluke' 1950 reverse against the US, the implications could not easily be dismissed.

Hidegkuti hit a hat-trick, including a first-minute 20-yarder, while right-half Bozsik chipped in with a stormer from outside the area. One of Puskas' two goals, a gem which sent the usually implacable Billy Wright sprawling, was memorably described by *The Times'* Geoffrey Green: 'Wright was like a fire engine arriving too late for the wrong blaze.' Describing Hungary as 'a side of progressive, dangerous artists who seem able to adjust themselves at will to any demand,' Green also pointed out that 'English football can be proud of its past, but it must awake to a new future.'

Another man on whom it made a deep and lasting impression was right-back Alf Ramsey. 'I have had one ambition hanging over me for years,' confessed the future England team manager some 10 years later, 'to replace the image of that great Hungarian side with the image of an even greater England team. From that time everybody has judged football by those wonderful Hungarians. I think this England team could do it. No, I don't just think. I *believe*.' He may have won the World Cup – but his team of triers never eclipsed the Hungarians' style.

When the World Cup returned to Europe in 1954, there were many critics who believed it a foregone conclusion that Hungary would translate their superiority into gold. Just three weeks before the competition finals, Hungary annihilated England 7-1. And when Poland withdrew, they were even spared the formality of qualification. Once in Switzerland, they were included with West Ger-

ABOVE: *Hungarian goalkeeper Grosics saves a Stanley Matthews' shot in their 6-3 win over England at Wembley in 1953.*

LEFT: *England defender Johnston shepherds the ball back to goalkeeper Merrick under pressure from Hungary centre-forward Hidegkuti.*

LEFT: *England captain Wright (left) watches anxiously as Merrick foils the Hungarians at Wembley. Full-back Ramsey (on goal line) later claimed the Hungarians as an influence on his World Cup winning team of 1966.*

BELOW LEFT: *England received another drubbing in May 1954 when they travelled to Budapest and were beaten 7-1. The picture shows Puskas (dark shirt) notching Hungary's third.*

BELOW: *England captain Billy Wright avenged the Hungarian beatings at club level when his Wolverhampton Wanderers team overcame Honved in 1954.*

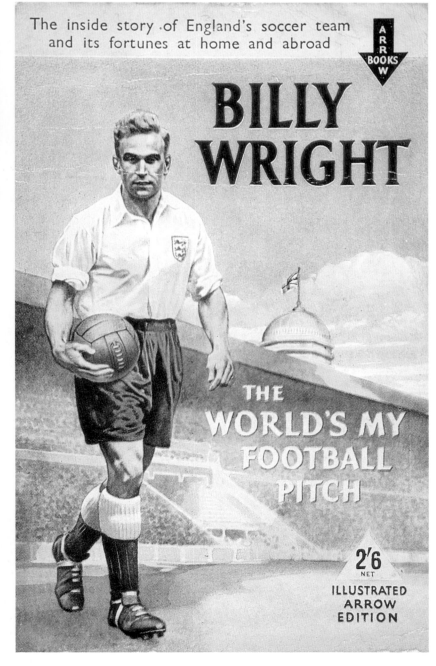

The inside story of England's soccer team and its fortunes at home and abroad

ARROW BOOKS

BILLY WRIGHT

THE WORLD'S MY FOOTBALL PITCH

2'6 NET

ILLUSTRATED ARROW EDITION

many, Korea and Turkey. In a once-only arrangement it was decided that the two strongest (or seeded) members of the four four-country pools would not play each other – a decision that, because it reduced the number of games and increased the probability of ties, led to further complicated rules and regulations being introduced. Extra time was to be played at the end of each drawn game, with play-offs between teams who ended up equal on points. Uruguay and their 1950 opponents Brazil were obviously forces to be reckoned with, the only question mark being acclimatisation. Scotland (for the first time) and England (for the second) were also present. Germany was on the up, Austria slightly on the decline, while Italy was in a state of transition.

Hungary's 17 goals in a mere two games seemed ominous enough – but an injury sustained by Puskas against Germany was to prove of longer-term importance. Germany's manager Sepp Herberger had understood the significance of the group system, and fired the first shot in a crucial battle of wits. Having already beaten Turkey 4-1, Herberger realised that he could afford to lose a game providing he won the play-off against Turkey. He therefore fielded six reserves against Hungary and saw his makeshift team on the wrong end of an 8-3 scoreline. This gave Germany the element of surprise in any future confrontation, while Korea's 9-0 drubbing by Hungary was scarcely a surprise. Germany beat Turkey as planned by 7-2 to confirm their place in the knock-out quarter-finals.

Scotland's 1-0 defeat against Austria was followed by news of the resignation of manager Andrew Beattie, frustrated at having his hands tied by a selection committee. The predictable result of the announcement was a seven-goal reverse at the hands of Uruguay. Beattie had been the first national manager. A story, apocryphal or otherwise, has a selector remarking to the players, 'Never mind lads, as long as we beat the English next April.' England, who had appointed Walter Winterbottom eight years earlier, won through to the quarter-finals, Billy Wright having moved to centre-half from wing-half due to an injury crisis. This was to prove a master stroke that extended Wright's career and influence for both his club and country (he won a record 105 caps). Even so the team went out to Uruguay 4-2, the game in which Stanley Matthews made his last World Cup appearance.

The most eventful quarter-final was that pitting Brazil against Hungary, a fixture that proved memorable for all the wrong reasons. Even the injured Ferenc Puskas had his behaviour called into question, with one newspaper alleging he struck a Brazilian player with a bottle. On the pitch, referee Arthur Ellis was obliged to dismiss three players.

Hidegkuti's third-minute opener set the tone; he was forcibly divested of his shorts while en route to scoring. Kocsis's less-revealing second after eight minutes seemed to settle matters, until a penalty permitted Djalma Santos to reduce the arrears. Lantos replied in kind to restore the Hungarians' two-goal cushion in a second half littered with fouls. But just as the stage was set for a dramatic climax after Julinho's mazy dribble and shot, tempers boiled over. Bozsic and Nilton Santos were dismissed for fighting.

ABOVE: *Hungary met their match in the 1954 World Cup Final where they were defeated 3-2 by West Germany in that country's first postwar World Cup. Rahn here scores his first goal.*

LEFT: *Uruguay's goalkeeper Maspoli punches clear under Hungarian pressure in the 1954 World Cup semi-final. Hungary's 4-2 win was the South American champion's first reverse.*

Kocsis settled matters – in footballing terms, anyway – in the 89th minute with his second goal, although Brazil's Tozzi still contrived to get himself dismissed for kicking before the long-awaited final whistle. Neither team punished their players, while the World Cup Disciplinary Committee remained similarly unconcerned. All in all a shameful 90 minutes of World Cup football.

Hungary again met South American opposition in the semi-final but, with the eyes of the world upon them via television (making its first visit to the competition), they played their part in a classic. With Puskas still missing, Uruguay had the better chance on paper of making their second successive final, but a scoreline of 4-2 in Hungary's favour does not reflect the evenness of a battle that lasted into extra time. Kocsis's two goals proved crucial. It was the first time Uruguay had been defeated in a World Cup fixture. In the final, Hungary were on the wrong end of a 3-2 scoreline, this time at the hands of West Germany. At full strength after a 6-1 drubbing of Austria in the semis, Herberger's team shaded it after a high-scoring first half left the score at 2-2. Morlock and Rahn (2) secured the Cup after Puskas and Czibor replied for the Hungarians. It is interesting to note that this was the fifth final out of five that the winning team had been from the continent in which it was held. This advantage was not to be overturned until the following tournament held once again in Europe, this time in Sweden.

INTO EUROPE

When English clubs were banned from Europe *sine die* in the aftermath of 1985's Heysel tragedy, it brought home most forcibly how European competition had broadened the minds and honed the skills of spectators and players, not to mention the national authorities, in just 30 years. Prior to the European Cup, the only way club sides could gauge their own prowess in international terms was by invitation matches, such as those played in England in 1945 by Moscow Dynamo and the much-publicised one-off game played in 1954 between Wolves and Honved. On running out 3-2 victors, Wanderers were dubbed 'Kings of Europe' and even 'Champions of the World' by a euphoric press still reeling at the Hungarian national team's undoubted superiority over their own.

The governing body of such competition, the European Union of Football Associations (initially known as EUFA, now, through the initials of the French styling, UEFA) was formed in 1955 under the secretaryship of one Henri Delaunay. It was no new idea, an unofficial predecessor being the Mitropa Cup dating from 1927, but it was the first to be officially sanctioned. As so often, however, FIFA and UEFA had to be goaded into action, in this case by the French sports paper *L'Equipe*, whose Gabriel Hanot had taken exception to the furore surrounding Wolves' win. The European Champions' Cup was born. Even had Wolves been the reigning champions of England, and not Chelsea, they would have been denied the chance to put their claims to the test, since the FA myopically advised the club not to take part. The initial 16 entrants were not all, in fact, national champions, but from the following season only such clubs would be eligible. Had they entered, Chelsea would have had little chance of beating Real Madrid, the team whose five-year grip on the Cup established them as a legend. Hibernian of Scotland were the UK's sole representatives. They reached the semi-final and emerged with a healthy profit of £25,000.

The next European club competition to come to fruition was the Inter Cities Fairs Cup, which got off to a very slow start indeed. The concept was to take players from all of a city's clubs to form a representative side but, as such a move was certain to play havoc with the domestic fixture schedules, the first tournament was spread over three seasons. Little wonder Barcelona's eventual 8-2 aggregate victory over a London select team hardly caught the public's imagination! The second Fairs Cup took two years before the tournament changed course and became an annual event for

RIGHT: *Crowds admire the European Cup Winners' Cup. First contested in 1960-61, it was the third of the major European club competitions to be initiated.*

individual clubs. Spain dominated the Cup's first years, with Barcelona (three times), Valencia (twice) and Zaragoza (once) all winners in space of the first eight competitions. Then England exerted a similar stranglehold as the Cup metamorphosed into the European Fairs Cup (1966). In 1971, Barcelona beat Leeds to win the trophy outright. Thenceforth a new trophy, the UEFA Cup, took its place. Qualification depended on finishing high up in the domestic league, each country having a quota of places.

Slotting in betweeen the UEFA and Champions' cups came the Cup Winners' Cup, open to winners of UEFA member countries' domestic cup competitions. The organisation of the 1960-61 tournament was devolved to the Mitropa committee, that precursor of the European Cup having recently been briefly revived, but when

ABOVE: *Manchester United manager Matt Busby was the first English manager to defy FA advice and take his club into Europe: his reward was a semi-final appearance before Munich decimated his team.*

RIGHT: *Italy score against Bulgaria in the 1968 European Football Championship, first contested in 1960 as the European Nations Cup and played in alternative years to the World Cup itself.*

RIGHT: *The tragic scene at Munich airport in 1958, where a great Manchester United side was ripped apart while flying home from a European Cup tie against Red Star Belgrade.*

the potential entrants swelled from 10 to 23, UEFA took charge in its usual 'decisive' fashion.

Like all other European club competitions, Cup Winners' Cup games were played on a home and away leg basis. The first final was also played in this fashion, with Rangers losing both legs to Fiorentina of Italy. They lost to Bayern Munich in 1967, but were finally to win it five years later, playing a part in the British domination that saw Tottenham, West Ham, Manchester City and Chelsea take the trophy between 1961 and 1972.

One of the most romantic aspects of the Cup Winners' Cup remains the participation of clubs whose pedigree and indeed ability would have ruled them out of either of its two sister competitions. The Welsh Cup, for example, occasionally yielded non-League winners, and it was Bangor City, the first of these to qualify, which beat mighty AC Napoli 2-0 at home in 1962-63. Had they been playing four years later, their 1-3 defeat in Naples would have seen them qualify on away goals, but as it was they succumbed 2-1 in a play-off.

English clubs had been dragged kicking and screaming into Europe by Sir Matt Busby and Manchester United. His lead in defying the FA ruling and taking United, League champions in 1956 and 1957, in search of greater glory, resulted in a semi-final against Atletico Bilbao in the first season, but backfired tragically with the 1958 Munich air crash. Before that cruel blow, they were well placed to repeat the feat, having overcome Red Star Belgrade in the quarter-finals. But AC Milan showed no charity in a 5-2 aggregate win.

Another important European competition to be instituted in the Fifties was the European Nations Cup. It had been one of UEFA's earlier concepts, but only in 1957 did the member countries get behind it and create a competition to take place every four years between World Cups. Each competition is known by the year of the final stages, even though the competition begins two years previously. The original format was a two-legged home and away tournament with the semi-finals and final played in a host country, but from 1980 onwards the World Cup model was used, with Italy holding a final tournament for the eight best teams. Russia were the first European Nations champions, beating Yugoslavia in a dour contest in France in 1960. Only 17 countries took part, the absentees including the four UK Home Countries (unsurprisingly), Italy and West Germany. The 1964 Cup saw entries up to 29, and the semi-final and final matches held in Spain. Russia once more made it to the final, but were beaten 2-1 by the home team. After this, the competition changed its name to become the European Football Championship.

THE 1950s LEAGUE

The Fifties was the decade in which English football, so often self-centred and inward looking, was exposed to world scrutiny. And while Wolves, with their three League wins in 1954, 1958 and 1959, were undoubtedly a great team, it soon became evident that their defeat of Hungary's crack Honved side by 3-2 in December 1954 was not enough to make them kings of the world. After all, the national team had taught England a double lesson at Wembley in November 1953 and on home soil six months later. Newspaper headlines of 'World Champions' were clearly an attempt to level those scores. Wolves achieved their aims through teamwork, winger Johnny Hancocks (who scored a penalty against Honved) one of the players in their side whom television would make near household names.

Nevertheless Wolves, rebuilt by Stan Cullis from the 'Team of the Forties' and captained inspirationally by England's Billy Wright, were indeed a class side. Hancocks and Jimmy Mullen were swift wingmen, while wing-halves Bill Slater and Ron Flowers were the engine room of the side. When Billy Wright retired after 499 appearances, his place was taken by George Showell. Their game was the long ball to the wing, then a centre for Roy Swinbourne or Jim Murray to connect with head, foot or chest. Goalkeeper Bert Williams, meanwhile, was a reliable custodian. Though the Wolves' long-ball game took them to three championships, Barcelona's 5-2 win at Molyneux in the European Cup of 1959-60 suggested that it was no match for continental guile. The same season saw Wolves narrowly miss the double, beating Blackburn to take the Cup but losing out

RIGHT: *Seen here captaining England, Billy Wright was also an inspirational club skipper for Wolverhampton Wanderers, leading them to three League championships in the Fifties.*

on a hat-trick of League honours by a single point. Wolves' style contrasted vividly with the push-and-run style fostered by Arthur Rowe at Spurs who had taken the title in 1950-51 but had fallen away thereafter. Their renaissance to finish second to Manchester United in 1957 was but a foretaste of the dominance to come.

United, meanwhile, finished top of the table in 1956 and 1957, the 'Busby Babes' showing the talent that flowered so briefly. Duncan Edwards of that side became the youngest player ever to wear a full England shirt when he was capped at the age of 18 years and 6 months against Scotland on 2 April 1955. Blackpool, Burnley and Preston all enjoyed their last real tastes of First Division power in this period: Preston running up to Wolves in 1958, Blackpool to Manchester United two years earlier and Burnley actually winning the championship in 1959-60. It was their second championship in 72 years, the other having been in 1921. The arrival of freedom of contract and the lifting of the maximum wage combined to make it impossible for such clubs to hold on to their stars. Another factor came with the inexorable rise of Manchester United. Their success, combined with the newly built motorways, often made it quicker and easier to reach Old Trafford than their local team. Bolton, Blackburn, Stockport and Bury were among the other clubs to suffer.

The 'retain and transfer' system was abolished in 1961 when George Eastham, then with Newcastle United, was refused a move. The idea that a player had to wait until a club wished to transfer him had never been challenged in a court of law until then. Although Eastham was not attacking the maximum wage as such, the 'retain and transfer' system had been very much part and parcel of the deal. Once a player had the right to decide his own destiny, it would only be a matter of time before clubs would be vying for his services with handfuls of pound notes. Eastham secured his victory with the help of Jimmy Hill and Cliff Lloyd, Chairman and Secretary respectively of the players' union, the Professional Footballers Asso-

ciation. The formal High Court ruling was reserved and finally delivered in 1963, ironically two years after the League had bowed to the inevitable and scrapped the system.

At the top end of the footballing scale, the most obvious sign of a revolution was the return from lucrative foreign exile of the likes of Denis Law and Jimmy Greaves. At home, Fulham's Johnny Haynes became the first £100 a week footballer, while clubs in the lower divisions soon accepted that they would have to get the best price for their top players rather than keeping them. This started a nursery system that exists to this day – and Fulham, who as a First Division club were able to accede to Haynes' demands, are now one of many nurseries for top clubs. Internationals Paul Parker (QPR) and Ray Houghton (Liverpool) were just two players sold to balance the books in the late Eighties.

Some clubs were forced to make swingeing cuts, even to the extent of scrapping a reserve team. The cost of running a football club was certainly not falling, while the abolition of regional football in 1958 had actually increased them. Amazingly, only Accrington Stanley went to the wall, but it seemed unlikely at that point that 92 full-time Football League clubs would be able to survive.

LEFT: *Johnny Haynes, the first £100-a-week player and a midfield maestro for Fulham and England.*

ABOVE: *Jimmy Greaves wins a rare header in England's colours. Noted for his close-in finishing on the ground, he signed for Spurs for £99,999.*

THE BUSBY BABES

In the postwar years, despite the successful runs of the likes of Liverpool and Leeds, there has only been one club to command loyalties countrywide, enthralling and enlisting as fans people who had never been within 100 miles of their ground. That team is Manchester United. Their fame and fortune was due to the strength and vision of one man – Scotsman Matt Busby, who had played for Manchester City and Liverpool as well as captaining his country before taking the hot seat at United in 1945.

The United success story started with the 1948 Cup-winning side. Busby had inherited players like Irish international Johnny Carey, Jack Rowley and Stan Pearson from the prewar team. To these stalwarts, he added players like right-winger Jimmy Delaney to produce a side of perfect balance. Carey was the mainspring, operating from right-half or right-back. The versatile Irishman played in every outfield position bar outside-right for United and seven times for his country. His instruction to 'keep playing football' even when his team were a goal down to Blackpool at Wembley when that first Cup was won 4-2 became legendary. Captain of the Rest of Europe against Great Britain in 1947, he was British player of the year in 1949 and turned successfully to management after his playing days were over.

The job of rebuilding that team led Busby to evolve the squad system, looking not only to create an 11-man team but also to provide a stream of ready-made replacements for its individual members by developing a flourishing youth policy. His own experiences had led him to fear for the future of young players 'left on their own – no-one taking any interest', or the situation of 'the first team hardly recognised the lads underneath, and the manager was a man sitting at his desk you saw once a week.' Thus the 'Busby Babes' were born. They might have added the FA Cup in 1957 and thus taken the double for only the second time this century, but goalkeeper Ray Wood was injured in the final against Aston Villa.

Despite a plucky performance by makeshift goalkeeper Jackie Blanchflower, there were no substitutes allowed in those days and the strain of playing with 10 men was too much, Villa winning 2-1.

Purchases of star players were the icing on the cake. Busby's success can be measured in five championship wins in 15 years – in 1952, 1956, 1957, 1965 and 1967. The eight-year gap between the third and fourth wins – the legacy of Munich – is as ugly as a missing tooth. The Munich air crash of 1958 took the lives of eight of their greatest players and tore the heart out of the 'Busby Babes'. It was all the more tragic in that a mere two years earlier Busby had been brave enough to defy the Football League and mount the first English assault on Europe. The League had hitherto persuaded English clubs to stand aloof.

The team had been playing Red Star Belgrade in a European Cup tie. A stopover in Munich in wintry conditions led to the Airspeed Elizabethan crashing on take-off for England after three attempts. The indelible image of the airliner's blackened frame, tail pointing vainly at the sky, will remain on all football fans' minds – and none will forget where they were or what they were doing when they heard the news. It was a tragic echo of the 1949 crash that cost the lives all but one of the AC Torino team which had played a friendly in Portugal. Duncan Edwards, Roger Byrne, Tommy Taylor, Bill Whelan, Geoff Bent, David Pegg, Mark Jones and Eddie Colman were the players who died. Busby himself was so badly injured he was given the last rites. Assistant manager Jimmy Murphy was absent on international duty, having been appointed part-time Welsh manager the year before. Returning to Old Trafford after a World Cup match at Cardiff against Israel, he saw the newspaper hoardings and went immediately to Busby's hospital bedside. 'Keep the flag flying, Jimmy,' said Busby, and Murphy did. Of the injured players, however, three were never to play again.

ABOVE: *Charred metal amid the snow as rescuers take the Manchester United team to hospital after the 1958 Munich disaster.*

FAR LEFT: *Emergency goalkeeper Jackie Blanchflower is beaten by Villa's second and winning goal in the 1957 FA Cup Final. The defeat deprived United of the double.*

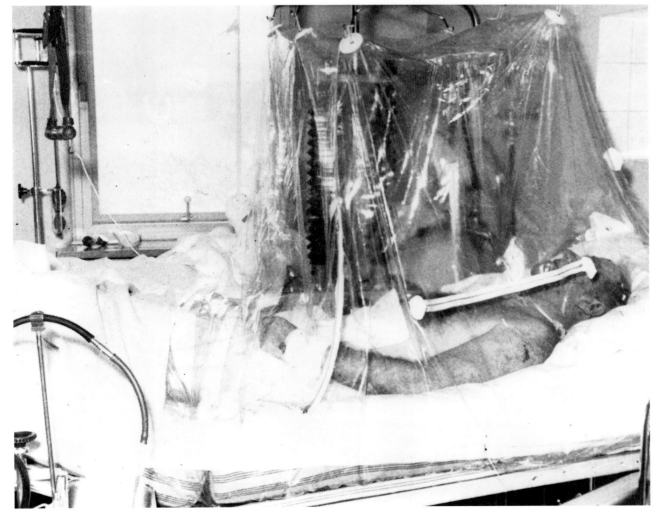

LEFT: *United manager Matt Busby pictured in an oxygen tent in the aftermath of the crash. Despite serious injury, he exhorted assistant Jimmy Murphy to 'keep the flag flying'.*

LEFT: *The patched up Manchester United squad after Munich. Shay Brennan (top, far right) and Bill Foulkes (centre front) were to play a part in the team's eventual European success.*

RIGHT: *Bobby Charlton in full flight, wearing United's unfamiliar blue change strip.*

BELOW RIGHT: *Enigmatic Ulsterman George Best, one of the most naturally gifted players to grace the Football League, whose career was blighted by personal problems.*

BELOW: *The first match after Munich – United beat Sheffield Wednesday 3-1, 20 February 1958.*

Their next League game against Sheffield Wednesday was deferred until 19 February, 10 days after the crash. Every place was left blank in what is now an historic match programme. In the event, Murphy bought just two players – Ernie Taylor, a Cup winner with both Newcastle and Blackpool and Villa's Stan Crowther, choosing to fill the remaining places with reserve or A-team players. 59,848 spectators saw United's emotional 3-0 win – a figure actually below Old Trafford's capacity, since the tens of thousands surrounding the ground with no hope of entry blocked the access of those who already had tickets.

The rapidly rebuilt team reached the Cup Final, but despite a wave of popular sympathy, lost to two goals from Bolton and England centre-forward Nat Lofthouse. United's second consecutive final was again dogged by controversy involving the Manchester goalkeeper. Bolton had established a tenuous one-goal lead and were clinging to it despite huge United support when a challenge between Lofthouse and Gregg ended with the goalkeeper in the net. Given the subsequent 'cotton-wool' protection accorded goalkeepers in such circumstances, it is a goal that would certainly not have been allowed even 10 years later, but in 1958 it sealed a most unpopular victory.

Three players who survived were to play prominent parts in the

glory to come. Harry Gregg, the Irish international goalkeeper, Bill Foulkes, once a coal miner from St Helens, now the sturdy stopper centre-half and Bobby Charlton, a rangy winger with an explosive shot recruited from the fertile breeding grounds of the Northeast. Born in 1937, he made his United debut at 19, scoring twice. Initially groomed as a centre-forward, he was to find greatest success as a deep-lying left-winger, moving forward for powerful two-footed strikes on goal. A youth policy had already paid dividends for United bringing them the FA Youth Cup for an unprecedented five years in succession. The net spread far and wide: witness Charlton, a Northumberland lad. The Irish connection was strong too, as a youngster from Belfast called George Best was soon to emphasise. Born in Belfast in 1946, he joined United at 15, but soon succumbed to homesickness. Two years later he was a fixture both in the city and the team. Like Bobby Charlton, he had developed his left foot by wearing a carpet slipper on his good right foot, while his speed and body swerve complemented his ball control to perfection. Making his debut at the start of the 1963 season, his confidence bordering on arrogance was evident even then. 'I knew then what I'd always believed – that I'd find it easy to play in the First Division.'

Busby's tactics were to play a short-passing game, utilising the midfield passing skills of stars such as Pat Crerand, short on pace but long on craft, who was fed with the ball by the tigerish Nobby Stiles. This contrasted markedly with the dominant long-ball philosophy that Wolves had used to such good effect in the late Fifties.

Home-bred players were mixed with established stars. Busby's biggest coup was to bring Denis Law back to Manchester despite spirited opposition from Arsenal. Law had started his career with Huddersfield before finding fame in 1960 with United's Maine Road rivals City. His feats included six goals in an abandoned FA Cup tie. A spell in Italy with Torino in 1961 didn't work out, and Busby had little hesitation in breaking the £100,000 barrier to repatriate him a year later. It was an inspired move, Law's quicksilver finishing and deceptive heading ability making him the ideal man to convert the chances created by the overlapping Charlton and Best. Law was the final piece of the jigsaw. The stage was set for further greatness.

WORLD CUP 1958

The 1958 World Cup Finals took place in Sweden. Fifty-one countries entered for the qualifying competition, but four of these withdrew without kicking a ball in anger. This competition was also noteworthy in being the first in which the Soviet Union participated. Encouraged by their victory in the 1956 Melbourne Olympics, they fielded a strong side with the legendary Lev Yashin a cornerstone in goal.

From a British standpoint, the competition was notable in that all four Home Countries – England, Wales, Scotland and Northern Ireland – were competing for the first time. As with Italy in 1950, England had been stripped of some of their greatest players by an air crash, in this case the infamous Munich accident earlier that year in which eight Manchester United players lost their lives. England's Roger Byrne, Tommy Taylor and Duncan Edwards perished, and though Bobby Charlton survived he was not to play a game in Sweden after a disappointing warm-up match. England had lost that game against Yugoslavia 5-0 but were still rated most likely to succeed in Sweden – despite Northern Ireland's superhuman effort in eliminating World Cup giants Italy. Under the management and captaincy of Peter Doherty and Danny Blanchflower respectively, the team made the most of the talents at its disposal which included a future national manager in Billy Bingham. Wales' arrival in Sweden had rather more luck to it. Israel's opponents having withdrawn on political grounds, Uruguay had then been selected from the group runners-up at random to play them for a final place. When they declined, Wales were next out of the hat and triumphed. Scotland qualified at the expense of Spain.

Hungary were, sadly, a mere shadow of their former all-conquering selves, the 1956 revolution having seen the defection of Kocsis, Czibor and Puskas. France were dark horses, Madrid's Raymond Kopa and Just Fontaine their stars. Fontaine (real name Kopaczewski) was the son of a Polish miner. He was the playmaker with an ability to split defences with his Haynes-like passing ability. Of the South Americans, Argentina had lost many talented youngsters to the Italians and were forced to rely on experience alone, while Brazil brought the exciting yet unpredictable gifts of Pele, a gifted 17-year-old carrying an injury, and Garrincha, a tricky winger known as 'Little Bird'. They played 4-2-4, a system admirably suited to Didi, the inside-forward whose 'falling leaf' free kick saw Brazil past Peru in the qualifying competition. (Ironically, he would return to the World Cup arena in 1970 as Peru's manager.) Didi ensured the four-man attack saw plenty of the ball, adding his lethal shooting power from set pieces to their already formidable armoury. In defence, Nilton Santos was an outstanding left-back.

France were the first to show with a 7-3 trouncing of Paraguay, three of these goals falling to Fontaine. Northern Ireland beat Czechoslovakia 1-0, but crashed 3-1 to Argentina. Scotland held Yugoslavia 1-1 and Wales drew with Mexico by the same score. Yet with goal average irrelevant, all but Scotland of the Home Countries made it to the knockout stage. Ominously, however, Brazil had Pele fit and Garrincha in their side, while Czechoslovakia took Argentina apart 6-1, yet did not even qualify, losing 2-1 to Northern Ireland. The Irish could not repeat their supreme effort against 4-0 victors France, while even Wales' giant goalkeeper Jack Kelsey was no proof against a single moment of Pele magic despite a gutsy play-off win against Hungary. Pele, born in the state of Minas Gerais in 1940, has just claim to be regarded as the world's greatest ever player. Just five foot eight inches tall and under 11 stone in weight, his heading ability was nevertheless legendary, due to a combination of good jumping and timing. (This was proved by an amazing headed goal in the final.) With perfect balance, he could ride most tackles, although a higher than average incidence of injury proved he was to be very much a marked man in international football from this World Cup on.

LEFT: *Brazil's 'Little Bird' Garrincha battles for possession against uneven odds during his side's 5-2 win against World Cup hosts Sweden.*

RIGHT: *Pele (right) rises with Swedish keeper Kalle Svensson during the 1958 final. The 'Black Pearl' notched two goals in a highly entertaining game.*

LEFT: *The victorious Brazilians acknowledge the Swedish crowd by carrying their national flag. Their 5-2 victory had been the most emphatic and entertaining ever in a World Cup.*

Brazil and France faced each other in a Stockholm semi-final that saw all Brazil's talents flowing together for the first time. A 5-2 victory included a hat-trick from Pele, who might have rivalled his opponent Fontaine's scoring prowess had he been fit from the outset. As it was, Fontaine added four goals in the third place match to one of France's two in the semi to make him the highest scorer ever in a World Cup Final with 13 goals. France's opponents in that consolation game which they won 6-3 were Germany, beaten 3-1 by the host country in Gothenburg. Swedish fans aside, however, there was little doubt as to the likely outcome of the final, won 5-2 by Brazil in a dazzling display. Vava (2), Pele (2) and Zagalo hitting

back after a shock fourth minute goal from Liedholm.

Mario Zagalo, nicknamed 'Little Ant' for his phenomenal and very un-Brazilian work rate, dropped to midfield to combat the Swedish threat – a move later claimed as pioneering the 4-3-3 formation so successful in the Sixties. With the experienced and imposing Djalmar Santos playing his first game in defence, the bustling Hamrin-Skoglund strike combination had little chance to shine thereafter, the game being killed as a competition – though not as a spectacle – with Brazil's third, volleyed by Pele after an overhead flick that left the crowd breathless. Like the 1958 World Cup, it had been a spectacle to savour.

PLAYING THE GAME (3)

Ironically, one of the men plotting the downfall of English tactics as pioneered by Herbert Chapman between the wars was himself a centre-half. Arthur Rowe was no conventional stopper when he played for Spurs. His coaching in Hungary in the late Thirties helped sow the seeds of a footballing revolution. 'There was no hint of what the Hungarians would later achieve,' he confessed, 'and yet in 1953 they had the finest team in the world.' The tactics of that team which journeyed to England and took them apart was based on the theory of the deep-lying centre-forward. Hidegkuti, wearing nine, was withdrawn into midfield, where Blackpool's Harry Johnston followed him, marking man for man. The pivoting full-backs Ramsey and Eckersley, did little more than play the oncoming Hungarian inside-forwards onside as they profited from the vacuum left by Johnston's absence. With long, penetrating balls played through by the likes of Boszik, the defence was hopelessly compromised.

This tactic was not the only reason England perished – the world class players in the Hungarian line-up had something to do with it too. But it inspired the concept of zonal defence, the idea that players would mark areas of space rather than specific men. Had England adopted this, Hidegkuti would have been picked up by a wing-half leaving Johnston to block the thrust down the middle. This concept was developed by Brazil into the 4-2-4 formation, with four men across the back marking space. The central two covered each other, the full-backs stayed wide. Although Brazil were a superb attacking team, this encouraged the line of four to act in concert, updating Billy McCracken's offside tactic and creating an area of dead space behind them that did much to stultify the game in the Eighties. The English game was still taking time to catch up as Manchester City player (and future England manager) Don Revie

proved by replicating Hidegkuti's success in season 1955-56. 'As the centre-forward I was the responsibility of the centre-half,' he later explained. 'Players and managers were chained to straight up and down attitudes.'

Brazil's 4-2-4 won them two consecutive World Cups. A back line of four found the centre-backs covering each other rather than Chapman's way of the full-backs pivoting to cover the middle. The full-backs now kept tight on the wingers, denying them time to pick up the ball and advance with it. With four attackers, their opponents' usual three-man defence found itself suddenly outnumbered, obliging the team to themselves play four at the back. This had ramifications later in the 'pressing' game where the back line moved up to the halfway line at every opportunity in an attempt to catch the opposing forwards offside. (A player cannot be offside in his own half.) This often meant that play was restricted to the middle third of the field. The system of the full-backs marking men and centre-backs marking space was a mixture of two systems, man for man defence and zonal defence. As English clubs entered Europe, so European standards began to affect the domestic game. Goalkeepers in Europe were accorded the greatest protection, so shoulder charging became a thing of the past. Likewise, the tackle from behind was discouraged.

BELOW: *England going down 6-3 to Hungary at Wembley. Here goalkeeper Merrick keeps the Hungarians at bay.*

REAL MADRID

Real Madrid – the prefix stands for Royal – were granted their title in 1920 by King Alfonso XIII, 22 years after being formed by a group of students. Forty years later, they stood as the undisputed rulers of European football with five European Cup wins to their credit. The seeds of that greatness were sown by centre-forward Santiago Bernabeu, whose playing career from 1912-1926 was just the start of a great association between man and club. Elected President in September 1943, he was the driving force behind the magnificent stadium that bears his name, and, having built this, he attempted with manager Jose Villalonga to assemble a team fit to grace it. And this they did. Their team – Puskas, Santamaria, Gento, Di Stefano – were individuals who combined to deadly effect. But it was Di Stefano, an Argentinian signed in September 1953, whose 11-year, 219 League goal career is remembered as the greatest of all. His strike rate in European competition was unparalleled, with 49 goals in 59 games, three of which were notched in the 1960 final. No wonder Spain adopted him and picked him to play 31 internationals in their colours!

No less a judge than Matt Busby remarked after viewing Real in 1957 that 'I have never seen a better player than Di Stefano.' Since then, his name has often been uttered when people discuss the greatest individual player of all time. Unlike other pretenders to the throne, Di Stefano rarely exhibited the whole range of his skills, preferring to bring Puskas, Gento and other fine runners into play – something he was well able to do in his preferred deep-lying centre-forward role. His ability to steal forward at the vital moment to strike at goal was a bonus. He called the shots, and the team responded.

On the debit side, perhaps, there was only room for one Di Stefano in a team – a point proved when Frenchman Raymond Kopa and the Brazilian Didi were bought, then discarded as their skills clashed with the master's. Alongside Di Stefano, Hungarian exile Ferenc Puskas seemed somewhat lacking in physical grace – but once in possession his skills were positively breathtaking. He had, of course, already come to the football world's attention as one of the masterful Magyars who had put English football well and truly in its place at Wembley in 1953. Fleeing his home country after the revolution, he signed for Real in 1958 when many considered him a veteran well past his prime – but he built up an understanding with Di Stefano that bordered on the telepathic. By the end of their first season together, both players were on 22 goals and at the top of the League listings. In a memorable moment, as the referee prepared to blow for time in the very last fixture, Puskas (in possession) bore down on the goalkeeper with his striking partner clear in front of goal. The Hungarian checked, sent the goalkeeper sprawling, then passed across the goal face for his waiting 'rival' to net. Puskas played for Real for seven years scoring 151 goals, 36 in European competition. By the time of his arrival at the Bernabeu, however, Real had already inscribed their name on the European Cup no fewer than three times.

Behind these high scorers lay a resolute defence marshalled by Uruguayan Jose Santamaria. Like Di Stefano, he was to represent Spain after joining Real in 1958, despite having played for the country of his birth in the 1954 World Cup. His Spanish parentage

BELOW: *The great Alfredo di Stefano put Real Madrid on the way to the last of their five consecutive European Cup wins at Hampden Park, Glasgow, in 1960. Eintracht Frankfurt are the opponents.*

may have been the reason for this. Known as 'The Wall' due to his physical stature, his size belied his skill.

Real's opponents in their first final in 1956 were Reims, by no means France's glamour club. They were inspired by international star Raymond Kopa, whose spirit nearly saw an upset. Madrid scraped home 4-3, later buying Kopa. He helped them overcome Reims again and win the following year, but returned to his former club in 1959, his talents incompatible with Di Stefano's and obliging him to remain out of the thick of the action on the right wing. 1957 saw the Italians of Fiorentina offer the last obstacle to the all-vanquishing Madrid machine, fortuitously playing in front of their home crowd. A first round stalemate with Rapid Vienna had occasioned a third match, again luckily staged in Madrid. On the credit side, Real had already brushed aside Matt Busby's mighty team on a 5-3 aggregate in the semi-final, a rather more impressive performance than Fiorentina's single goal against Red Star of Belgrade. And so it proved, Di Stefano (penalty) and Gento netting without reply as thousands of jubilant Spaniards celebrated the retention of the European crown.

The 1957-58 campaign was particularly fruitful, with Madrid picking up the championship and Latin Cup. But European success remained the prime objective, and their goal tally reached new heights . Their path to a meeting in Brussels with AC Milan included victories over Antwerp (aggregate 8-1), Seville (10-2) and Vasas Budapest (4-2). The final was won 3-2 in entertaining fashion. 1958-59 saw Puskas added to the forward line to take part in goal-scoring feats against the hapless Irish of Drumcondra (13-1) and Austria's Weiner SK (7-1), before an altogether trickier proposition – a Madrid derby against Atletico – raised its head. A 2-2 aggregate necessitated a playoff in the neutral Spanish city of Zaragoza, where Real ran out 2-1 winners. Reims, Raymond Kopa's old club, were the opposition in Stuttgart, and goals from Mateos and Di Stefano ensured the Frenchman ran out a winner in his last European final with his adopted club.

The 1960 final against Eintracht Frankfurt in Glasgow will always be remembered for its spectacular 7-3 scoreline. Four of the goals came from the irrepressible Puskas, three from Di Stefano in a two-man show that had the Hampden crowd roaring. And they had double reason to: Eintracht had hit Rangers for six in both legs of their semi-final. Ahead at half time (3-1) after the Germans had the impudence to take the lead through the veteran winger Kress, the Spaniards hit three more in quick succession after the interval. Stein pulled it back to 2-6 and added a consolation third after Di

Stefano, alone, had completed his hat-trick. It was quite a swan-song. Another highlight of 1960 was the first World Club Championship, a cup to be contested between the champions of Europe and South America. Their opponents were Penarol of Uruguay. A 0-0 draw having been achieved in Montevideo, Real triumphed 5-1 with almost insolent ease in the return, Santamaria outstanding against his countrymen. Real's European reign ended, ironically, in Spain – the victors Barcelona. Drawing 2-2 in the Bernabeu, Real travelled the short distance to the Nou Camp knowing their chances were less than even. The 2-1 scoreline on the night (a 4-3 reverse in aggregate terms) tells only part of the story, no fewer than three Real goals being disallowed. Barcelona went on to lose to Benfica, the eventual winners. By that time, Real could boast an unbeaten record over 20 ties (aggregate score), having scored 112 goals and conceded 42.

An attempt to rekindle the European dream ended sadly in 1961-62. For the first time in seven seasons an opposing club won in the Bernabeu – and though Juventus were made to pay when Real defeated them in Italy, the final clash against Benfica was not so successful. Staged in Amsterdam, the game brought together the European Cup's only holders to date. The stage was set for a thrilling climax, and the crowd was not disappointed when Puskas notched two quick goals. Benfica levelled, only for the portly Hungarian to defy time, space and his waistline to complete his hat-trick. But the goalscorer in the ascendancy was Eusebio, and the Portuguese striker's two late goals brought the trophy back to Lisbon. Puskas gave the youngster his shirt after the game, some observers seeing this as a symbolic transfer of the mantle of footballing greatness.

Real's last final appearance with the classic team followed two seasons later, when Inter Milan rebuffed their challenge in Vienna. The end was merciless: Di Stefano departed on a free transfer after 11 years' service, joining Espanol. He later became a successful manager both in Spain and South America, and returned to Real in that capacity in 1982. Puskas (who later managed Panathinaikos of Greece to the 1971 European Cup Final) and Santamaria faded from view – and though Gento and Pachin survived from the 1960 team to take the trophy in 1966 after a win over Partizan of Belgrade, the golden era was over. The decade of 1956 to 1965 saw Madrid write their name on the Spanish Championship no fewer than seven times, in addition to those five European wins and two further final appearances. They had also secured the World Club Championship on the one and only time they played for it.

RIGHT: *Di Stefano (left) admires a Juventus player's acrobatic scissors-kick. The Italians' surprise 1962 victory at the Bernabeu was the first by any European Cup opponent in seven seasons; Real won the play-off but lost in the final.*

ABOVE: *Real beat Juventus in a Paris play-off in the 1962 European Cup quarter-final. By this time, the Spaniards' mask of invincibility had well and truly slipped.*

LEFT: *Eusebio, the Benfica striker who hit two late goals to inflict Real Madrid's first European Cup defeat in the 1962 final.*

PART IV

The New Professionals

SUPER SPURS

William Nicholson, or 'Bill Nick' as all at White Hart Lane knew him, was probably the nearest that the South could offer to rival Matt Busby in terms of a universally respected soccer supremo. Although the League and Cup double won in the 1960-61 season inevitably overshadowed all his other achievements, his main attribute was consistency. After taking the manager's chair from Jimmy Anderson, he won the FA Cup three times, the League Cup twice, the European Cup Winners' Cup and the UEFA Cup. Following his first season, the team slipped below seventh place but once in the next 13 years. In addition, not one of his seven major finals was lost. Nicholson had played right-half in the Tottenham team that had won the Second and First championships in 1949-51 under Arthur Rowe. Their so-called 'push and run' style gained them many admirers. Another notable player in that team was full-back Alf Ramsey, later manager of England.

Nicholson took on the coach's job after his playing days were over, and was appointed team manager in 1958. His first match was a 10-4 victory over Everton. He built his team around the irrepressible Irishman Danny Blanchflower, coincidentally or not, a winghalf like himself. It was already obvious that the garrulous Blanchflower would enjoy a long career in the game as manager and sometime press pundit. At Spurs, his presence as captain and midfield general gave them almost two managers, one on the field and one in the stand. The team served notice of intent under Jimmy Anderson, Nicholson's predecessor, by finishing second and third in successive seasons as the Fifties closed. An unexpected drop to 18th in Nicholson's first season as manager was followed by another third place in 1959-60. Captain Blanchflower's taste for on-the-field control had led him to be dropped by manager Anderson, but Nicholson backed his captain and the result was a winning team. At 32, Blanchflower was in the autumn of his career, yet his authority and experience were invaluable. Nicholson clearly appreciated this. 'I gave him authority on the field,' said the manager, 'but told him to remember I had been responsible for the money paid out on the players and I took the responsibility for the results. So he must not knowingly go against my policy.' The relationship worked.

Nicholson bolstered the team he inherited with some great buys: three Scots, ball-winner Dave Mackay, playmaker John White and goalkeeper Bill Brown. Ironically Mackay was signed after Spurs had lost out to North London rivals Arsenal for injury-prone Welsh stopper Mel Charles, and in Arsenal coach Ron Greenwood's words, 'The also-ran turned out to be the real winner.' Johnny Brooks departed to Chelsea for Les Allen, a strong-running forward. He also developed the skills of full-backs Peter Baker and Ron Henry, and winger Terry Dyson, who had been all fringe players for some years but came good under Nicholson's shrewd man-management. All in all, Nicholson had assembled skilled ball players, strong ball-winners and a fast, fluid forward line that could look after itself. It was an all-weather team of classic proportions, helped by the fact that only winger Cliff Jones missed more than a handful of matches.

PAGE 68: *Shay Brennan (left) and Bobby Charlton display the European Cup at Wembley in May 1968 – 10 years after the Munich disaster.*

LEFT: *Victorious Spurs captain Danny Blanchflower poses with the League and FA Cup trophies after his team won the first double of the twentieth century in 1961.*

LEFT: *Blanchflower was given on-field authority by manager Bill Nicholson, and repaid his manager by displaying notable tactical awareness.*

BELOW: *Terry Dyson beats Leicester goalkeeper Gordon Banks for Spurs' second and last goal in the 1961 FA Cup Final – the match that clinched the double but marred by an injury to Leicester's Chalmers that left them with 10 men.*

LEFT: *Star striker Jimmy Greaves threads his way through the Liverpool defence. His addition to the double-winning side typified manager Nicholson's determination to perfect his team.*

The League Championship was won in impressive style in the following season, 1960-61, when an amazing goals ratio of 115 to 55 left them a full eight points clear of Sheffield Wednesday, the runners-up. They began the season with a record 11 successive wins, and ended it with another record – a total of 31 wins in 42 games. In later days of three points for a win, this would have seen them amass 97 points as opposed to the 66 they actually registered, the latter a total only equalled by Arsenal. No fewer than 16 of those wins were away from home – yet another record – while eight were consecutive. Tottenham reached Wembley certain of the title but, though the pressure was off, failed to acquit themselves with the style to which their fans had become accustomed. Nevertheless, their 2-0 victory against Leicester City, with goals from Smith and Dyson, ensured they wrote their name indelibly in the record books by being the first team in the twentieth century to win the League and Cup double. Over two and a half million spectators saw them do it. This success was not enough for Nicholson, who strengthened his side by bringing itinerant striker Jimmy Greaves back from a short and unhappy stay in Italy – helped in this by the recent abolition of the maximum wage. The former Chelsea player proved

ABOVE: *Centre-forward Bobby Smith tees up Spurs' first goal against Dukla Prague in the 1962 European Cup quarter-finals.*

LEFT: *Jimmy Greaves, perhaps the most lethal finisher in postwar League football. Alf Ramsey's' decision to omit him from England's World Cup team caused a furore.*

to be the icing on the cake and, along with Terry Medwin, propelled Spurs to a repeat Cup Final win, this time against Burnley, 3-1.

Spurs were the first British team to exploit the squad system, though Birmingham had in fact been first to win in Europe. They had cover in every position: two goalkeepers (Brown and Hollowbread), three full-backs (Baker, Hopkins and Henry), four half-backs (Blanchflower, the captain, Mackay, Marchi and Norman) and no fewer than seven forwards (Greaves, Medwin, White, Dyson, Jones, Smith and Allen). Medwin replaced Jones while the Welsh winger was absent injured. Their victory in the 1963 Cup Winners' Cup final in Rotterdam was decisive enough: a 5-1 defeat of Athletico Madrid, secured by goals from Greaves (2), White and Dyson (2) to an Athletico penalty. The win also opened the floodgates for British teams to make up for lost time in Europe, with West Ham, Liverpool, Rangers and Manchester City all finalists in the competition in the Sixties. Spurs players created a record on 12 October 1963 when seven were picked to represent their countries on a single day in the Home International Championship. Smith, Greaves and Norman (England) met Jones (Wales), while Brown, Mackay and White (Scotland) faced Northern Ireland. Nicholson returned to Wembley to take the Cup again in 1967, but his team hardly compared in overall quality to the double side. Pat Jennings in goal, midfield man Alan Mullery, and striker Alan Gilzean would have held their own in any company, but Greaves was past his peak. Spurs were relegated in 1977.

The glory days for Spurs failed to continue even though Terry Neill, Keith Burkinshaw and Peter Shreeve all tried to emulate past glories. Burkinshaw took the FA Cup in 1981 and 1982, while 1984 saw the UEFA Cup gained after a penalty shootout. But the League eluded all three, and Cup success (the FA Cup in 1981, memorably featuring Argentinians Ardiles and Villa) was not enough. The late

Eighties saw Spurs attempt to use the chequebook to recapture their influence, the hunger for success intensifying as deadly North London rivals Arsenal took the League title in 1989. Terry Venables, a former player in the 1967 Cup-winning side and tipped as a future England manager, was employed to produce a miracle, and he rekindled hopes by bringing England striker Gary Lineker back from his old club Barcelona. Lineker was teamed with Paul Gascoigne, an immature but precocious talent, although the third star in the Spurs firmament, Chris Waddle, departed for £4.25 million to Marseilles, allegedly to balance the books which showed an off-field loss.

FAR LEFT: *Osvaldo Ardiles who, with Argentinian compatriot Ricky Villa (left) brought a touch of South American flair to Tottenham in the early Eighties. Ten years later, Ardiles was manager of Swindon Town, while Villa, a Cup Final goalscorer in 1981, had returned to his native land.*

RIGHT: *England striker Chris Waddle poses in the colours of his new club Marseilles. His departure from Spurs in 1989 was the cause of much debate and disillusionment among supporters.*

WORLD CUP 1962

The 56 countries enrolling for the 1962 World Cup was five more in 1958. The finals were to be staged in Chile, the venue suggesting strongly that, having recently won in an unfriendly continent, Brazil were going to be hard to displace as holders. Their grip on the Cup was strengthened by the fact that players like Vava and Didi had enjoyed experience in Spain since the last tournament. They were able to boast nine of the side that had clinched the Cup four years ago. And among them was Pele. As a World Cup host, Chile followed tradition in promising opulent facilities and delivering rather less. Earthquakes had disrupted the pattern of life, and the fact that they managed to stage the competition at all was praiseworthy. England faced their fourth campaign with Walter Winterbottom in charge. Bobby Charlton had now succeeded to a team once again built round Fulham's playmaker Johnny Haynes. Bobby Moore was installed in the defensive wing-half position once filled by Wright, flanked by Huddersfield's deft full-back Ray Wilson. Together with Charlton, these were destined to be three vital cogs in the 1966 team.

As expected, the South Americans were the first to show: Chile, Uruguay, Argentina and Brazil were all early winners. England slipped up 2-1 against a Hungary team still striving to live up to the reputation of their forebears. Elsewhere, nationalistic fervour was threatening to sour the atmosphere. Hosts Chile subjected Italy to a torrid examination – and not only in footballing terms. Italy suffered a broken nose and two dismissals, while the Chileans remained unpunished despite their behaviour in a game English referee Ken Aston later deemed 'uncontrollable'. The Chilean victory, with two goals in the last 15 minutes, was predictable but unapplauded. England surprisingly beat Argentina 3-1 with the assistance of a penalty, while Hungary fired a warning shot with a 6-1 victory over Bulgaria, Albert hitting a hat-trick. Brazil's World Cup hopes were blighted in their second match, a draw against Yugoslavia. Not only did they fail to score, but Pele's appearance for only 25 minutes before succumbing to a torn thigh muscle ended his personal interest in the competition. Brazil scraped past Spain, now featuring Hungarian exile Ferenc Puskas, while Russia's humiliating 4-4 draw with lowly Colombia was a personal tragedy for Lev Yashin: the once-legendary goalkeeper gifted the opposition a vital second goal at 4-1 up.

Brazil cantered past England 3-1 in the quarters, Garrincha scoring twice and Amarildo filling Pele's boots to perfection. Their opponents in the semi-final were to be Chile, who succeeded where Colombia had run out of steam. The now sadly all-too-fallible Yashin was at fault for both long-range goals. Czechoslovakia had beaten Hungary 1-0 with a goal against the run of play, while Yugoslavia's 86th-minute goal accounted for Germany by a similar margin. The semi-final draw, however, ensured a Europe versus South America final. The all-South American game ended in acrimony when Garrincha, whose two first-half goals killed off Chile's hopes, was sent off for retaliation and was hit on the head with a bottle. Chile's Landa was also dismissed. By contrast, the Iron Curtain clash between Yugoslavia and Czechoslovakia attracted only 5000 spectators and was won 3-1 by the Czechs.

Having battled against the odds, the Czechs were clearly intent on making Brazil fight to retain the trophy. The two teams had met in their qualifying group, where a goalless draw must have given the Eastern Europeans hope. The match was set alight when the scheming Josef Masopust carved a hole in the Brazilian defence to open the scoring in the final. Could the form-book be overturned?

Pele's replacement Amarildo then came into his own, scoring one from an improbable angle, then centring for Zito to head past the hitherto heroic Schroiff. The keeper then dropped the ball at Vava's feet and it was all over.

This competition was widely regarded as the most disappointing of all World Cup tournaments to date. With little attractive football on show and far too many displays of cynical play, not least by the host country, it was hoped that England's tournament in 1966 would prove more of a footballing feast.

RIGHT: *Brazil's team pose before their 3-1 victory over Czechoslovakia.*

BELOW RIGHT: *Pele was the only link between the victorious Brazilian sides of 1962 and (pictured) 1970. His 1962 campaign, however, was foreshortened by a thigh injury.*

RIGHT: *Bobby Charlton, an England regular by 1962, could not help his country overturn Brazil, their quarter-final victors.*

THE LEAGUE CUP

The Cup, to any English fan, has one meaning and one meaning only – the Football Association Cup. The Football League in 1960 seemed to think so too – for instead of giving a new knockout competition their unanimous and unreserved approval they brought it into existence with a mere 15-vote majority. Thus was born the Football League Cup, a trophy later to be known by a variety of commercially-orientated names as it was offered for sponsorship to the highest bidder. Yet instead of dwindling and dying, the sickly child grew from strength to strength, perhaps aided by the fact that for four years it was sponsored by the health-giving Milk Marketing Board. When the home and away final was replaced by a day out at Wembley's twin towers, it was clear that this infant could no longer be confined to the lower orders, the attachment of a European

qualifying place having long since encouraged the bigger clubs to join in.

Five clubs had boycotted the competition in its first year of existence; a further five found it too much of a strain on a fixture list already full of European dates and the like to repeat the experience. Few outside the clubs involved paid much attention to the finals and in 1962, when Second Division Norwich beat Fourth Division Rochdale, the aggregate attendance of just over 30,000 suggested the supporters themselves had better things on which to spend their money. League Secretary Alan Hardaker, the iron-willed supremo who had taken the organisation by the scruff of the neck in 1957, made no bones about the fact that it was his hobby horse, but pointed out the fact that even the FA Cup struggled, in its earliest stages, to pull in the requisite number of entries. The tide turned in 1966, when the twin promise of Wembley and European qualification was introduced. The previous season had seen seven of the top eight First Division clubs staying out, including holders Chelsea who believed a fixture clash with the Fairs Inter Cities Cup would impair their chances of European advancement.

The first Wembley winners in 1967, Queens Park Rangers, were a Third Division side – but in a ding-dong 90-minute encounter their victory over holders West Bromwich by 3-2 was hailed as a David-versus-Goliath effort. Neither Rangers nor Swindon, likewise popular winners two years later by 3-1 over Arsenal, were permitted to

take up the European option, while Leeds, winners in 1968, would have qualified anyway through being fourth in the League. In both giant-killing cases, television made overnight heroes of goalscorers Rodney Marsh (Rangers) and Don Rogers (Swindon), permitting both to make big-money moves to larger clubs. The only teams to remain unconvinced were Merseyside giants Liverpool and Everton. But the lesser lights of the First Division like Stoke City needed no second bidding. Losing finalists in 1964 in the early years of the competition, they revelled in the Wembley atmosphere to beat Chelsea 2-1 in 1972 and register their first major honour in 109 years. Nobody could say their success hadn't been fairly earned, either, since the previous year's League meeting had passed a motion making it obligatory for all clubs to enter.

The years 1973 to 1975 saw a strange hat-trick from Norwich manager Ron Saunders. Having lost the 1973 final to a Ralph Coates goal for Spurs, he led new club Manchester City to Wembley the following year to lose again to Wolverhampton Wanderers. Having departed City in acrimonious circumstances, he derived some consolation in 1975 when he finally gained a League Cup Final win with Aston Villa – over Norwich! It was, in fact, to be the curtain-raiser to a five-year period of success for Saunders which would end with a championship win in 1981 and a European Cup win (after his departure) the following year. Villa returned two years later (1977) to fight a dour goalless draw with Everton. This final was the only one to take three games to settle, a Hillsborough replay ending 1-1 and a third match at Old Trafford in Villa's favour by the narrowest of 3-2 margins.

Nottingham Forest did their own double in 1977-78 and 1978-79, needing a replay to defeat Liverpool 1-0 after a second successive scoreless Wembley final, while their 3-2 triumph over Southampton was much easier than the scoreline suggests. Like Ron Saunders, Forest's legendary manager Brian Clough found the League Cup a prelude to European success though again in the European Cup rather than the UEFA Cup to which their League Cup win qualified his team. In 1982, the League Cup grasped the double-edged sword of sponsorship, becoming the Milk Cup – at which time it had already become a fixture in the Liverpool boardroom! Having scornfully snubbed the earliest years of the competition, the Merseysiders won four consecutive finals against West Ham (2-1, after a replay in 1981), Tottenham Hotspur (3-1), Manchester United (2-1) and rivals Everton (1-0, after a replay).

The Littlewoods Cup (as it was renamed) then reverted to the domain of the smaller clubs for a couple of seasons with Norwich picking up their second win in four appearances in 1985 thanks to a Sunderland own goal and a penalty failure by Clive Walker (only the second penalty miss ever in a Wembley final, and the first since 1913). Both clubs were later relegated from the First Division. Oxford caused a surprise by beating 1967 giant-killers QPR 3-0 before Arsenal and Notts Forest took the trophy back to the big boys' trophy cabinets. In 1990, Littlewoods announced they were ceasing to sponsor the Cup after the current season – and, while potential sponsors were far from scarce, the Football League insisted that connections with apartheid (South Africa) or alcohol were unacceptable. One thing was sure, however – that even (temporarily) without the plum of European qualification to attract the attention, the trophy that started life as the League Cup was as healthy as any 30-year-old, and was likely to remain a part of the English sporting calendar for the forseeable future.

FAR LEFT: *Brian Clough makes a point from the touchline.*

BELOW LEFT: *Liverpool celebrate their 3-1 victory over Spurs in the 1982 Milk Cup.*

BELOW: *Arsenal pose for the camera after their 2-1 victory over Liverpool in the 1987 Littlewoods Cup.*

WORLD CUP 1966

England staged the World Cup in 1966 – and, unlike many previous hosts, had the facilities to do it in some style. Nevertheless, the wish to maximise revenue saw England play all their games at the 100,000-capacity Wembley Stadium, a fact that didn't pass without comment from the other competitors. Walter Winterbottom, the FA's chief coach from 1946 to 1963, had been replaced as England team manager by Ipswich boss Alf Ramsey. Having taken his unfashionable club side to the League Championship in 1962, the new man was ideally placed to inherit the national side after another World Cup exit that year. His tactical acumen was generally recognised, although no-one could have predicted that the pattern of play he chose would be so influential – some would say detrimental – to the game in the two decades that followed. Among the contenders were North Korea, surprise 9-2 aggregate victors over Australia in the qualifiers after the other group members withdrew.

Adopted as their own by the Northeast crowd, they were clearly outsiders. Of the others, Uruguay (who held England to a goalless draw in their first match) were one quarter of a strong South American presence that included Brazil, Argentina and Chile. Portugal had an outstanding player in Eusebio, while Italy, potentially strong, left out captain Picchi, playmaker Corso and goalscorer Rivera. The Soviet Union retained Yashin despite his unhappy experiences in Chile four years earlier.

The biggest win of the opening matches was West Germany's 5-0 crushing of Switzerland, giving early notice of their intentions.

BELOW: *Making the draw for the 1966 World Cup held in England.*

RIGHT: *The official mascot for the 1966 competition – 'World Cup Willie'.*

WORLD CUP CHAMPIONSHIP

1966

WORLD CUP WILLIE

Beckenbauer was magisterial in midfield, with striker Uwe Seeler leading the line expertly. Brazil lost Pele for the second match, his second World Cup blighted through injury, and their loss in that game to Hungary proved crucial. Another reverse to the Portuguese followed, though the returning Pele suffered again at the hands and feet of Morais. In the final analysis, players like Bellini, Garrincha, Djalma Santos, Orlando and Zito were past their best, and the 21 players used in their three games could not be totally explained by injuries.

England's two 2-0 wins against Mexico and France were achieved only by dint of some effort, and Ramsey's team plans looked far from accomplished: midfield hardman Nobby Stiles drew criticism from high places for one particular foul during the France game. Two Football Association officials demanded his replacement, but Ramsey stood firm. It was a turning point. Another turning point was reached at Middlesbrough when North Korea, having drawn with Chile, deservedly beat Italy by a single goal. It was enough to take them to the quarter-finals and ensure that Italy's manager, Fabbri, would find himself unemployed at the end of the tournament. Korea's progress was halted by Portugal, though not before the hint of another surprise when they stormed into a 3-0 lead. Eusebio proved the matchwinner, however, turning on a dazzling display of individual skill. Four goals – two from the penalty spot as the Koreans lost their self-control as well as their self-belief – plus another from Augusto brought the Portuguese safely through, much to their evident relief.

Two Uruguayans were dismissed as they crashed 4-0 to Germany, who went through to meet fellow semi-finalists Russia. England played in an equally dramatic Europe-South America quarter-final clash at Wembley. The result, a single goal win through newly-introduced striker Geoff Hurst, became almost in-

FAR LEFT: *Sir Alf Ramsey, England's victorious manager in 1966.*

BELOW, FAR LEFT: *North Korea celebrate their second goal against fancied Portugal. The Koreans lost a thrilling match 5-3.*

LEFT: *England on their way to a 1-0 win over Argentina in the quarter-finals.*

BELOW: *The Argentines lose their captain Rattin, ordered from the field for a second bookable offence of dissent.*

cidental when Argentine skipper Antonio Rattin declined to leave the field when dismissed for dissent, a second bookable offence. The hitherto implacable Alf Ramsey's description of the Argentines as 'animals' describes the remainder of proceedings admirably. He was to find no such fault with Portugal, who were unfortunate not to emerge with a draw in their semi-final encounter. Though trailing to a brace of goals by Bobby Charlton, his brother Jack handled to present Eusebio with a penalty chance he accepted with alacrity. The resulting Portuguese pressure was only just resisted. In the other semi, Germany overcame Russia by the same score, having the fortune to play half the game against nine men after Chislenko's dismissal and Sabo's injury .

The final at Wembley was a home game in every sense for England – yet they contrived to throw away a hard-earned 2-1 lead at the last. Hurst's goal just before half-time equalised Haller's thirteenth minute strike, and Peters struck 13 minutes before the final whistle after a goalmouth scramble. The defender Weber, who was involved in that incident, levelled the scores after a dubious free-kick award from Swiss referee Dienst. With extra time following almost immediately, Alf Ramsey played his motivational trump card. Declaring that his team had won the World Cup once, he told them to go out and win it again. 'Look at them.' he cried, pointing at their opponents. 'They're finished.' And so it proved. But the deci-

sive blow, again from Hurst, was not without controversy. His right-footed shot from a Ball centre bounced down from goalkeeper Tilkowski's crossbar. Forward Hunt was on hand to drive home any rebound, but turned away, certain the ball had crossed the line – as, at length, was the Soviet linesman when consulted by the referee. Hurst's third goal and England's fourth was scored while the Germans threw everything into attack. It settled the result but not, for some, the argument. To Hurst, a West Ham squad player a few months before, fell the honour of the first hat-trick in a World Cup Final.

Portugal beat Russia for third place 2-1, yet another Eusebio penalty deciding things. But the Portuguese style of football, building their team round that player's silky skills, contrasted greatly with the functional football with which England had attained their victory. Everything had gone right for Ramsey, who was knighted for his achievement; even the critics, who had sniped at the omission of the prolific Greaves, were forced to eat their words when his replacement Hurst hit his historic hat-trick. England would have to settle for third place in the European Championships of 1968, the title going with Italy's home advantage (1-0 against Yugoslavia), but with the World Cup once again switching continents neither England nor Italy could be confident that the South American eclipse was anything other than temporary.

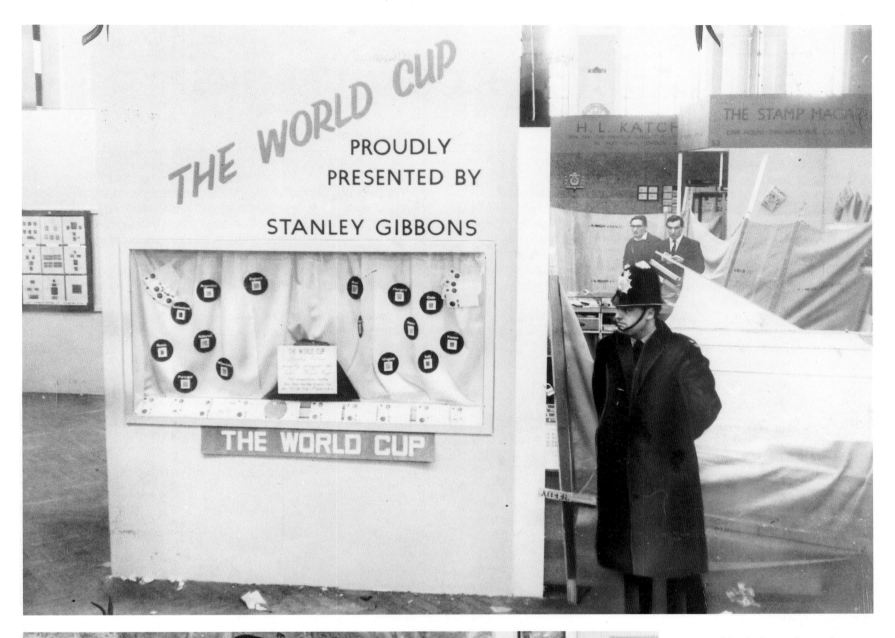

FAR LEFT: *Martin Peters (centre) celebrates his World Cup final goal. West Ham team-mate Geoff Hurst supplied the others in a 4-2 extra-time win.*

ABOVE: *The display case from which the World Cup was stolen in March 1966. An explanatory notice fills the gap.*

LEFT: *Pickles, the dog who sniffed out the World Cup eight days after its theft from Westminster's Central Hall.*

CELTIC THE CONQUERORS

As a nation, Scotland's international football reputation had never been high. The occasional victory in the annual clash with England was more than eclipsed by their humiliating 9-3 Wembley defeat in 1961. They missed out on World Cup qualification more often than not, a gap from 1958 to 1974 being enough to confirm the fact. But Celtic's triumph in the 1967 European Cup Final under legendary manager Jock Stein put Scottish football on the world map in no uncertain terms.

Stein had played for Celtic after beginning his working life in the coal pit. He moved on to non-League Llanelli in Wales after three years at Parkhead. Returning north of the border in 1954, he was approached by Celtic to re-sign as reserve team player-coach, helping their youngsters attain first-team maturity. That was the plan – but injuries to two senior defenders pitched Stein back into the first team for a famous League and Cup double. He joined Dunfermline as manager in 1960, inspiring a spirited and successful fight against relegation and taking them to the Scottish Cup Final in 1961 where, as fate would have it, they met Celtic. Another against-the-odds win, this time 2-0 after a goalless draw, ensured Stein would return to Parkhead as manager, which he duly did in March 1965 after a successful period at Hibernian. Stein had built his team not around one player but several. Billy McNeill, the craggy centre-

RIGHT: *Tommy Gemmell's long-range shot nestles in the back of Inter Milan keeper Sarti's net, the first goal in Celtic's European Cup victory.*

LEFT: *Police protection for one of three Celtic players dismissed during the World Club Championship game between Celtic and Racing Club of Argentina. The latter finished the game with nine men.*

LEFT: *Celtic central defender Billy McNeill wears the blue shirt of Scotland in 1967.*

BELOW: *Twenty-two years later, McNeill surveys Parkhead as he enters his second spell of management with his former club.*

half who was twice to manage the club in Stein's wake, veteran goalkeeper Ronnie Simpson, midfield schemers in Bertie Auld and Bobby Murdoch and the lionhearted Bobby Lennox up front were all crucial figures – not to mention a potential Best-like match-winner in winger Jimmy Johnstone.

Celtic were the first British team to reach the final stage of the competition, and had already achieved a clean sweep of Scottish honours. Their path to the final in Lisbon saw them beat Zurich, Nantes, Novi Sad and Dukla Prague. The team they were to meet, Inter Milan, had (with city rivals AC) taken on the mantle of European Cup invincibility with wins in 1963 (AC), 1964 and 1965 (Inter). Celtic's all-action style seemed likely, if anything could, to shake the Italians' self-assurance, already dented when Spanish-born inside-forward Luis Suarez was ruled out through injury. Despite losing an early goal to a sixth-minute Mazzola penalty, the 'Lisbon Lions' held firm. Pressing constantly to crack the Italians' famed defence, they came back in the second half with goals from Gemmell (a spectacular long-range effort) and Chalmers to win 2-1. Though they could not repeat their European triumph the following year, Celtic's League win had started a nine-year tenure, eclipsing Rangers record of three wins in four years. In 1970 they reached the European Cup Final once more only to play disappointingly in a 2-1 extra time loss to Holland's Feyenoord.

Scots club managers like Stein, Busby and Bill Shankly clearly didn't relish the challenge of the national team (although Stein had tried the job on for size on a part-time basis after ex-Rangers man Ian McColl was sacked in 1966). Following him was John Prentice of Clyde, who barely had time to change the office name-plate before he was out in six months. Bobby Brown, formerly Rangers keeper, preceded Tommy Docherty en route to Manchester United. Willie Ormond presided for the relatively successful 1974 World Cup, Ally McLeod for the disastrous 1978 one. When Jock Stein eventually took the job after an unhappy spell at Leeds, it was clear he had taken it 10 years too late.

Back on the club front, Rangers brought a second European pot to Glasgow when they beat Moscow Dynamo 3-2 in 1972. Played in Barcelona, the victory was marred by crowd trouble but confirmed that Scottish football had more to offer than its national side sometimes suggested. That aside, Rangers' victory presaged a national revival which saw them unbeaten in the 1974 World Cup Finals in Germany.

Rangers, with Jim Baxter in superb form, took three titles in four seasons before Celtic's European Cup win heralded an unbroken nine-year grip on the League. As the title changed hands in 1974-75 – inevitably to Rangers, delighted to foil their rival's hoped-for tenth title – the Scottish League was restructured to reduce the First Division to 10 clubs. Now titled the Premier Division, it headed a League structure of Premier, First and Second Divisions, the latter of 14 clubs apiece. With just one club promoted and relegated from the top flight, it was clear the existing elite were on to a good thing – not to mention the fact that with teams meeting twice at home and twice away to make up the fixture numbers, they could be assured of four, not just two, Glasgow paydays each and every season.

The Old Firm's domestic domination was broken by Aberdeen in 1980 and in 1983 by Dundee United. Having sharpened their skills against European opposition and reached the quarter-finals of the UEFA Cup twice running, United took the championship against the odds on the final day of the season. One of their closest challengers was Aberdeen – yet despite missing out on the title, they put even United's effort in the shade with their own double – Scottish Cup and Cup Winners' Cup. A victory against Bayern Munich in the quarter-finals made Europe sit up and take notice of Alex Ferguson's men – and the campaign was concluded successfully by beating hot favourites Real Madrid (managed by that European legend Alfredo Di Stefano) on a rainy night in Gothenburg. In conditions in which they were clearly at home, and with no fewer than 10,000 supporters – some of whom had put to sea in the city's fishing fleet – in the 18,000 crowd, they beat the Spaniards 2-1. The scoreline tells only half the story, however, the Dons scoring through Black in six minutes, then fending off a Real fight-back after a Juanito penalty in the fifteenth minute. Extra time saw the Scots' stamina triumph, with substitute Hewitt using his fresh pair of legs to glance home his fifth goal of the competition.

The game proved the springboard for further honours – the League and Cup double in 1984 and the championship retained in 1985. Many of the team then left to further their careers elsewhere – Leighton and Strachan followed manager Ferguson to Manchester United, McGhee went to Hamburg, Rougvie to Chelsea and Weir to Luton. But with the League win of Dundee United, 1983 had been the year the pendulum swung away from the Old Firm and towards the lesser lights of Scottish football. A counter-revolution, assisted by Ibrox boss Graeme Souness's chequebook, was still to come.

UNITED: 10 YEARS ON

As Manchester United progressed through the Sixties, it seemed their destiny to play for the European Cup in whose quest eight young lives had been lost back in 1958. In 1965, as Football League champions, United had tried for the third time to take the trophy – only to fail in, of all places, Belgrade. Playing Red Star's city rivals Partizan in the semi-finals, they lost not only the tie (2-0 there, 2-1 on aggregate) but also George Best, who sustained a cartilage injury that required an operation.

United had won the previous year's championship against strong opposition in Leeds. Unfortunate to go down 2-1 at Wembley against Liverpool after extra time, Don Revie's emerging team were level on points with United but with an inferior goal difference. The following season's domestic competition saw Leeds once again runners-up to Liverpool, with United fourth behind Burnley. The 1966-67 season saw them back on top and ready for another tilt at the ultimate prize.

They were not to be the first British club to take Europe's top trophy: Celtic had beaten them to that accolade. But as they moved past Hibernians Valletta (4-0), Sarajevo (2-1) and Gornik (2-1), their destined final place looked in jeopardy when they scraped a narrow 1-0 win against those European pace-setters of the Fifties in front of their own Old Trafford crowd. And all those fears were made manifest when Real took a 3-1 lead in the Bernabeu. But they had rescued the tie against Sarajevo by winning 2-1 away after a goalless first leg. And spurred by the prospect of a final at Wembley – a second home for most of the team – they hit back through David Sadler and the Munich veteran defender Bill Foulkes to equalise the scores on the night at 3-3 and take them through on the narrowest

of 4-3 aggregates – all this after being 2-0 and then 3-1 down. Foulkes, the former coal miner from St Helens, epitomised the fighting spirit that had taken the club back to the top.

The final, against Eusebio's Benfica was unusual for two reasons – a colour clash that saw United playing in unfamiliar blue shirts and the absence of the mercurial Denis Law, with his great experience of European football, through injury. His replacement, a young 19-year-old called Brian Kidd, was relatively untried. Nevertheless, 'home' advantage saw United installed as favourites, and with a wave of 10-year-old emotion to sweep them home the result looked assured. Busby himself was smiling as 100,000 fans – nearly all United supporters for a day – roared his name in unison.

As so often in football, however, this was not the way the game went. Bobby Charlton scored with what was a rarity for him, a glancing header, but it was no surprise when Benfica levelled. At 1-1, goalkeeper Alex Stepney brought off one of the saves of his life to deny Eusebio, leaving United grateful for the chance of another strength-sapping 30-minute stretch on the lush Wembley turf. Their superior stamina prevailed as extra time wore on, and goals from George Best, the young Brian Kidd and a final strike from Bobby Charlton in one of the greatest of his many superb Wembley

BELOW: *David Sadler's cheeky back-heel into Real Madrid's net helped ensure a European Cup Final place for the Old Trafford team in 1968.*

RIGHT: *Captain Noel Cantwell with the FA Cup, won 3-1 by United against Leicester City in 1963.*

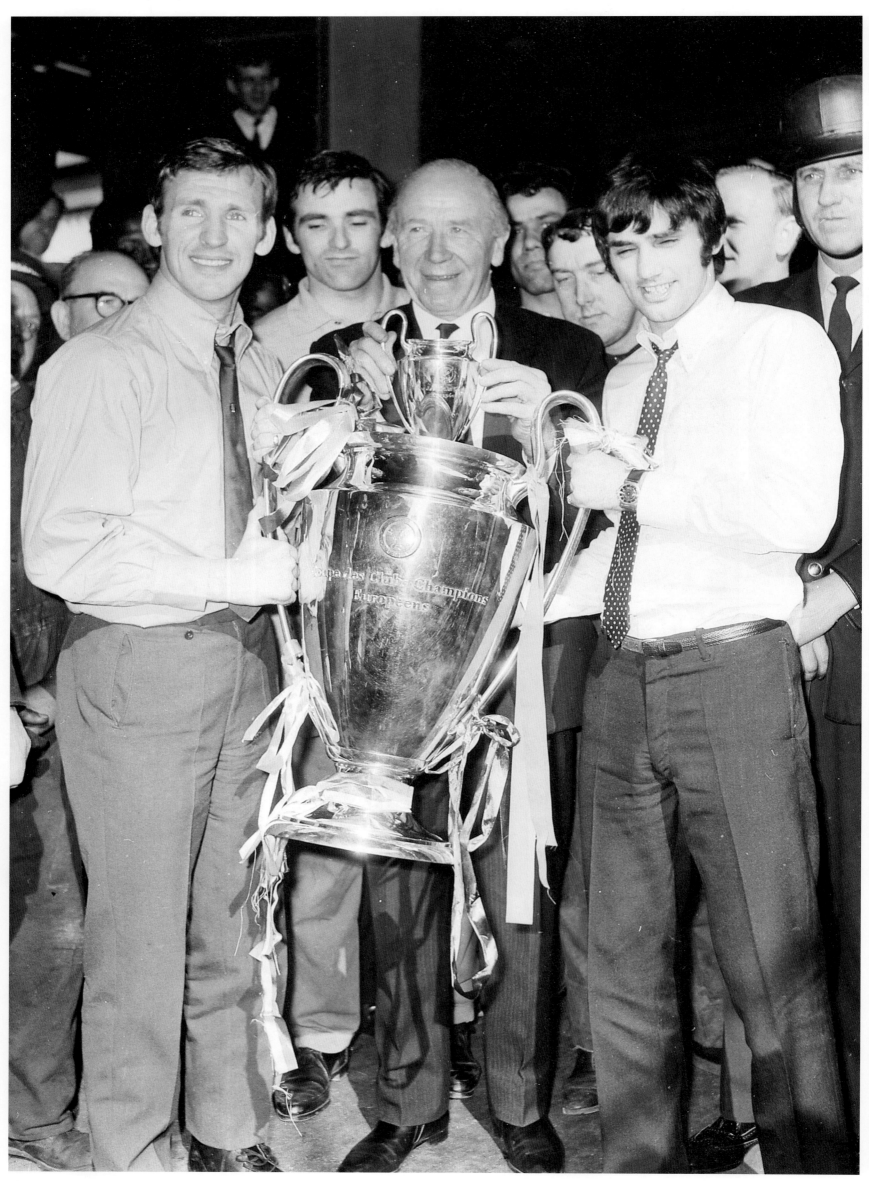

performances saw them safely home. Best's goal was the pick of the match, darting infield to pick up the ball after a Stepney goal kick eluded a Benfica defender, then rounding a defender, drawing the keeper and slotting home into what was by now an unguarded net. The victory banquet was attended by the parents of those whose death in Munich would never be forgotten. And significantly Bobby Charlton was absent from the festivities, mindful of those who could not join them: Roger Byrne, David Pegg, Eddie Colman, Tommy Taylor, Bill Whelan, Duncan Edwards, Mark Jones and Geoff Bent.

Of the Cup-winning team, Law was to enjoy a last spell at the top with Manchester City, ironically scoring a goal that doomed United to relegation. He returned to the Scotland team for the 1974 World Cup Finals, playing against Zaire to bring his total caps to 55. Best was lost to the game, drink and a penchant for pretty girls doing most effectively what defenders had found impossible. He went on to Los Angeles Aztecs in the NASL, Fulham, Hibernian and Bournemouth but failed to return to anything like his old form – a tragedy for him and his country, who finally attained the World Cup Final stage in 1982. It was too late for Best. Bobby Charlton was to retain his links with the club by becoming a director, after a brief attempt at management at Preston had proved unsatisfactory.

The award of a knighthood to Matt Busby was one of the most popular and deserved honours ever bestowed on a character in the game. His final record stood as follows: five championships (runners-up an additional seven times), two FA Cups (twice beaten finalists) and, of course, the European Cup. Their defence of the latter went as far as the semi-finals in the 1968-69 season when they fell to eventual winners AC Milan. Sadly for the man and his club, the decision to hand over the reins in the summer of 1969 was to herald an era of doubt and dissent at Old Trafford. Initially, the appointment of reserve team boss Wilf McGuinness – himself a product of Busby's youth policy in the Fifties – seemed a sensible one. But with Sir Matt retaining influence and authority as General Manager, McGuinness's reign was to prove a brief one. He swiftly returned to the reserves, replaced brusquely and without ceremony by Leicester's Frank O'Farrell whose 18-month tenure coincided with George Best's fall from grace. The player's departure to Los Angeles in 1972 effectively ended an era, and more or less coincided with O'Farrell's own farewell.

FAR LEFT: *Manager Matt Busby savours the European win with players Pat Crerand (left) and George Best (right) as they take the trophy back to Old Trafford on the day after their Wembley triumph.*

LEFT: *The award of a knighthood to the Manchester United manager in 1968 was one of the most deserved awards in professional sport.*

The Irishman's successors, Tommy Docherty (1972-77), Dave Sexton (1977-81), Ron Atkinson (1981-86) and Alex Ferguson (1986-), all proved unequal to the task of bringing the title back to Old Trafford. Each however had his highspots: Docherty surrounded himself with a team of Scots, yet took the team down to the Second Division – returning in triumph a year later. His departure the day after United had defeated Liverpool in the FA Cup Final coincided with the revelation that he had run off with the physiotherapist's wife. An introvert by nature, Sexton was appointed as the antithesis of the ebullient, headstrong Docherty. Despite proving costly in the transfer market to little immediate effect, he could consider himself unfortunate to be sacked after ending the 1980-81 season with a club record of seven successive wins. Gates had declined under his tenure, while neighbours City had flamboyant characters like Malcolm Allison and John Bond at the helm.

Atkinson won the FA Cup twice, in 1983 and 1985, on the latter occasion denying Everton the remarkable treble of League, Cup and Cup Winners' Cup – even when down to 10 men after the sending off of Kevin Moran, the first in a Wembley FA Cup Final. But when Cup form failed to translate into League supremacy (third in 1983, fourth the following three seasons) he went. Ferguson arrived, having put Aberdeen on the Scottish football map – and promptly cleared out 13 of the 22-strong squad in two years. Yet even surrounding himself with Scots like Docherty didn't work out: Jim Leighton, his Aberdeen keeper, proved an unreliable custodian. He brought back star striker Mark Hughes from Barcelona, where he had been an expensive failure, and with a £2.5 million overdraft at the start of the 1988 season it was clear Ferguson would have to sell to buy again.

But it was more significant that Liverpool, who financed Ian Rush's similar re-signing from Juventus from their reserves, were now Britain's best supported club. In February 1990, Ferguson found he had equalled the unwanted record set by Frank O'Farrell's team of 1971-72 of 11 games without a win. With boardroom uncertainty – Chairman Martin Edwards attempted unsuccessfully to sell the club to unknown businessman Michael Knighton, much to the distress of players, fellow directors and supporters alike – it seemed the image of Manchester United was an increasingly tarnished one, despite a 1990 FA Cup Final appearance.

FAR LEFT: *Tommy Docherty, a flamboyant and popular figure who nevertheless took the team down to the Second Division.*

LEFT: *Dave Sexton, unluckily sacked after ending the 1980-81 season with seven wins in a row.*

BELOW LEFT: *Ian Rush, Mark Hughes's Welsh striking partner at national level, was, like Hughes, brought back after leaving his club for a foreign side.*

ABOVE: *The gifted Hughes (left) leaves his team-mates standing. His return to United from Barcelona did not bring immediate dividends, however.*

LEFT: *Ron Atkinson, twice a Cup winner for United as a manager but never able to mount a sustained League challenge.*

FOLLOWING PAGES: *American dreamers – 38 Texan schoolboys arrive in England in 1969 to learn the rudiments of soccer. Unfortunately, the in-built American resistance to the world game was not to be easily overcome.*

95

AMERICAN DREAMS

Until the Seventies, all the world really knew of Association Football in America was their sensational World Cup victory over England in Uruguay in 1950, when a single goal by a forward called Albert Gaetjens inspired banner headlines. With the formation of the North American Soccer League (NASL) in 1968, all eyes were once again turned towards America as talented players from Europe and South America swelled the ranks, many arriving in the twilight of their careers. World Cup winning captain Franz Beckenbauer, Dutch dynamo Johann Neeskens, the incomparable Pele -these names and more inspired hopes that the Western world's biggest potential market for soccer was finally to be tapped. Such hopes turned out to be illusory when the stars departed and the NASL collapsed in the early Eighties. But the qualification of an indigenous American team for the 1990 World Cup and the long-awaited award of the 1994 final showed that all was not lost. But the roots of the game went back a lot further than many realised.

Soccer first came to the United States in the nineteenth century, with the first games played at colleges on the East Coast in 1830. The influx of immigrants from Europe at the turn of the century brought the game to the grass-roots in a curious parallel of the 'Gentlemen versus Players' situation in England. These immigrant communities rarely mixed with the college fraternity, who split their game into four 20-minute quarters and tried variations on the pitch. When the siting of the 1930 World Cup Finals in Uruguay dissuaded all but four European countries from taking part, the United States happily filled in. The team lined up as follows: Douglas, Wood, Moorhouse, Gallagher, Tracey, Brown, Gonsalez, Florie, Patenaude, Auld and McGhee. The derivation of the surnames tells all you need to know about the composition of the team: by and large British former professionals who had emigrated with the promise of money from the big US steel companies which had hoped to form a league. The team made it to the semi-finals, registering healthy 3-0 scorelines against Belgium and Paraguay. But a six-goal drubbing by Argentina brought their adventure to an end, and it was not until Brazil in 1950 that they would once again surprise the world with their prowess. As in 1930, a substantial proportion of that team came from immigrant stock, while captain Eddie McIlvenny and manager Bill Jeffrey were both Scots.

The win against England failed to set the game alight in the States – and while British teams often toured in the close season as a fundraising exercise, mostly watched by immigrant British and Italian fans, it wasn't until magnate Bill Cox funded an international soccer league in the late Fifties that the American public had even limited access to high-quality professional competition. Dukla Prague, West Ham and Kilmarnock were among the participants. Cox, who already owned a basketball team, clearly saw potential for the new sport and formed a National Professional Soccer League (NPSL) – which was immediately banned by FIFA! The NPSL kicked off in 1967 with 10 clubs, nine from the US and the Toronto Falcons from north of the border. Few British players would risk a FIFA ban by going, notable exceptions being Phil Woosnam and Vic Crowe, both ex-Aston Villa and Wales, and Northern Ireland's Peter McParland. Brazil's Ze Maria was a rare household name to take the plunge, but the playing staffs were brought up to strength not with American nationals but immigrants. Despite this, five-figure crowds were drawn for the first games.

Competition was not long in arriving with the FIFA-backed United Soccer Association importing a roster of European and South American clubs to adopt the name of the city at which they were based in a two-division summer competition. Inevitably, the two leagues merged in 1967, by which time NSPL gates had fallen to an average of around 5000 in the face of strong competition from the 'traditional' US sports of ice hockey, American Football and baseball. The resulting National League had the advantage of FIFA sanction, a fact that led leading coaches like Gordon Jago to try their

luck without fear of a world ban should the experiment fail. Jago who joined Baltimore Bays ended up assisting Phil Woosnam, one of the first NSPL imports and now US team coach, prepare the national side.

The North American Soccer League kicked off in 1968. Organisationally, the NASL followed American Football's lead with 16 clubs divided geographically into two conferences to minimise travelling. The Eastern conference comprised the Atlantic and Lakes Divisions, the Western conference the Gulf and Pacific Divisions. After the two conference winners played off to decide the representatives in the final, the championship would be decided on a two-leg, home and away basis. Atlanta, heading the Atlantic Division, beat Pacific leaders San Diego 3-0 on aggregate to become the first champions. Succeeding years saw the format or point-scoring of the competition change. Points were standardised as six for a win and three for a draw, with up to three further bonus points being available for each goal scored up to a maximum of three. Nine points was the most a team could take from any fixture.

1975 saw the introduction of Soccer Bowl, akin to the American Football Superbowl. A single match had settled matters since 1972: now it was time for razzmatazz. The venue for each year's Soccer Bowl would be determined in advance, leading to the possibility of a club having home advantage should they be fortunate enough to win through. In 1981, this led to the unlikely situation of Chicago and New York contesting the North American Soccer League in Canada – something akin to staging the FA Cup Final at Hampden Park,

Glasgow. Pele's arrival at New York Cosmos in 1975 really put the seal on the NASL's golden age. He was the perfect ambassador for the sport, respected by whites and a role model for blacks. He was far from the only import. The arrival of Johann Neeskens, the Barcelona and Holland midfield dynamo, at New York was especially surprising following his outstanding game for Barcelona in the 1979 European Cup Winners' Cup final. Germany's Franz Beckenbauer missed out on the 1978 World Cup, having already signed for the Cosmos. He returned to his native land to play for Hanover, returning for a final American summer in 1983 at the age of nearly 38. Cruyff, Beckenbauer's European sparring partner, also made it over in the twilight of his career to play for Washington.

Many British clubs were prepared to loan out their players in the close season to cut their wage bill, accepting the possible risk of injury and the chance that, should the American team be successful,

their players would have to miss the first few League games as the final stages of the NASL playoffs took place. Trevor Francis, soon to become one of Britain's most expensive footballers, was loaned by Birmingham City to Philadelphia in 1978. On his return, hard-up Birmingham wanted to transfer him to another English club, yet Nottingham Forest, the club which eventually signed him, were not keen for their expensive asset to be playing year-round and on bone-hard artificial pitches which could play havoc with a player's leg joints. Coventry City, whose chairman Jimmy Hill was very

BELOW LEFT: *Franz Beckenbauer ended the Eighties as Germany's team manager. Ten years previously, he had been trying his luck in the North American Soccer League with New York Cosmos.*

BELOW: *Johann Cruyff, one of the most gifted European players of the postwar era, left Holland to play for Washington.*

much involved investing in the NASL, put in a bid for Francis partly financed by summers in America – in effect hiring out an expensive asset for a period when Coventry could not use him. In the end, Hill and Coventry were to lose out on Francis and, with the Detroit and Washington franchises failing, British and American investors alike lost money.

While the NASL appeared to change its points system with un-nerving regularity, its allegiance to FIFA prevented too much tampering with the rules of play. One innovation that did make it, however, was a 30-yard area delineated by a line across the pitch. A player could not be offside outside this area, thereby reducing the effect of defenders 'pressing' to the half-way line and far fewer offside decisions. The NASL reached its zenith in 1978, when a 24-strong League in two conferences of three four-club divisions apiece was won by New York Cosmos. By 1982, also won by the Cosmos, its strength had been reduced by half. The writing was on the wall. The NASL survived one more season and splintered, the best players going off to indoor leagues. Yet that was far from the end of the story. The award of the 1994 World Cup seemed likely to rejuvenate the game's prospects. And with a home-grown team of undergraduates winning through to the 1990 finals in Italy, there was every chance that this time the razzmatazz of the professional game would find firmer foundations in the schools, colleges, parks and playing fields of North America. 'Ah,' said the cynics, 'haven't we heard that one before?'

BELOW: *Trevor Francis was one of many players to extend their earning power by playing in the States in the summer when the British season was finished.*

WORLD CUP 1970

The 1970 World Cup was played in Mexico, after a strong challenge from Argentina had failed. It followed the Olympics by two years, ensuring the existence of stadia and facilities but inviting a repeat of the problems of altitude and heat that especially affected European participants. The Olympic tournament final of 1968 had been contested by Hungary and Bulgaria, however, and proved it was possible that, with suitable acclimatisation, European players could prevail. Exacerbating this situation, however, was the insistence of television that many games kicked off at mid-day in temperatures of up to 100 degrees.

Brazil were many people's bet to take the Cup for the third time, despite a change of manager a few months before when Joao Saldanha, broadcaster, journalist and ex-Communist activist who had given the team a year's preparation with a world tour, was replaced by Mario Zagalo, left-winger in the victorious team of 1958 and 1962. It could have been an omen. Playing against three Europeans in England, Romania and Czechoslovakia they could be confident. Their ace player, alongside the incomparable Pele of course, was chainsmoking inside-left Gerson. Starting his career with Flamengo, he made his mark in the 1960 Olympics. By the time he

LEFT: *The fantastic Azteca Stadium in Mexico celebrates the opening of the 1970 World Cup with a display of balloons.*

FOLLOWING PAGES: *Jairzinho prepares to beat England goalkeeper Gordon Banks in the teams' 1970 World Cup clash. Martin Peters (11), like goalkeeper Banks a former winner, looks on.*

ABOVE: *Gordon Banks completes his miraculous save from Pele in the 1970 World Cup at the Guadalajara Stadium.*

RIGHT: *A meeting of midfield minds as Bobby Charlton of England (centre) encounters Italy's Gianni Rivera under the gaze of Gordon Banks.*

made the 1966 World Cup team he had passed through Botafogo to Sao Paulo, but this experience could not help him make a mark. In 1970, he was at his peak as a midfield general, ably supported by Tostao and Jairzinho.

England manager Alf Ramsey had been knighted for his achievements, but could not work the magic away from home soil. An acclimatising tour of Colombia and Ecuador was blighted by the (baseless) accusation against captain Bobby Moore of stealing a bracelet. His assured performances both on and off the field were praiseworthy. West Germany, out to go one better than four years previously, discovered in Gerd Muller a lethal finisher to play in front of Uwe Seeler, contesting his fourth World Cup from midfield. Italy now favoured Riva, the talented forward left out in 1966, while in Peru, coached by Brazilian Didi (twice a winner himself), the South Americans had a skilful, less petulant alternative to Argentina, the team they beat to reach Mexico. Israel and Morocco were the rank outsiders, the former's arrival due in part to North Korea's refusal to play them on political grounds.

The early group matches proceeded with few surprises, Russia and Mexico winning through from Group I. Italy and Uruguay, Brazil and England and West Germany and Peru emerged from the others. The highlight of this round had been the meeting of Brazil, twice former winners, and England, the team that had succeeded them. A sleepless night, thanks to the noise-making of mischievous Brazilian supporters, nullified the advantage of Gerson's non-availability. The game will live forever in World Cup history for goalkeeper Gordon Banks' amazing save from Pele's tenth-minute header. The centre from Jairzinho was inch-perfect, the downward header by Pele the perfect way to beat a goalkeeper in the air. Yet as the ball bounced up to hit the net just inside the post – and, with Pele already holding arms aloft in triumph – Banks flung himself full-length to somehow turn the ball over the bar to safety. Despite this world-class save, Banks was beaten in the second half by Jairzinho, although the defeat didn't affect their chances of qualifying. Belgium lost to a dubious fifteenth minute penalty awarded to the hosts, whose ultimate quarter-final appearance was the first of their World Cup career.

Quarter-finalists England and Germany replayed the previous competition's final in Leon, where England were victims of a double blow – one possibly self-inflicted. The first was that Gordon Banks, their outstanding goalkeeper, went down with food poisoning, ensuring understudy Bonnetti played his first competitive match in

Mexico in a crucial situation. Secondly, Alf Ramsey withdrew Bobby Charlton and Martin Peters in a double substitution to introduce fresh legs at a stage where England, having gone 2-0 up, still led 2-1. Extra time was secured by a Seeler header, but unlike 1966 the Germans now had the ascendancy. Muller's volley sealed it, but from the English point of view the substitution has always, fairly or not, been seen as the turning point.

Italy's progress was scarcely assisted by the rivalry between playmaker Gianni Rivera of AC Milan and Sandrino Mazzola, his counterpart with city rivals Inter. Rivera's two goals against Mexico in the quarter-final and winner against West Germany in the semi couldn't stop him being condemned to the substitutes' bench for the final. He played just six minutes. Elsewhere, Uruguay – without star player Rocha – squeezed past Russia with a disputed Esparrago goal in the dying seconds of extra time. The attractive Peru met their match in Brazil, Rivelino, Tostao (2) and Jairzinho negating Gallardo and Cubillas' strikes. Italy won their semi against Germany by the narrowest of 4-3 margins in extra time, Germany claiming a professional foul against Beckenbauer cost them the match. 1-1 at full time, the extra half-hour saw five goals scored – and with Helmut Schoen having used his substitutes, Beckenbauer's injury effectively reduced them to 10 men. Elsewhere, Brazil beat Uruguay 3-1 despite their opponents' cynical play.

The final was between two teams with the very best of World Cup histories. With two wins apiece, this was a true decider – winner takes all, with three wins obtaining the Jules Rimet trophy in perpetuity. Although the press reports indicate that this was Pele's match – he scored a great goal, made two and finally made up for the final he missed through injury in 1962 – it was dominated by Gerson. Fit again, he ran the midfield as he pleased and smashed the ball past Zoff from the edge of the penalty area to restore Brazil's lead after Boninsegna equalised Pele's majestic opening header. Jairzinho and, minutes from the whistle, the overlapping full-back Carlos Alberto set the seal on a famous victory. West Germany's 1-0 victory to secure third place hardly mattered in this carnival of South American flair.

SHANKLY'S SUPERMAN

'Football isn't a matter of life and death – it's *much* more important.' This, the most famous of the many colourful phrases coined by Scot Bill Shankly, sums up both football on Merseyside and the man himself. Manager of Liverpool from 1959 to 1974, his reign is celebrated to this day by the Shankly Gates at Liverpool's Anfield ground.

An abrasive wing-half, he had played with distinction for Preston North End and Scotland. His indomitable spirit on the field was recalled by team-mate Tom Finney who was exhorted in his first game to 'Keep fighting . . . we can do it yet' at four goals down with two minutes to play. Shankly returned to football after the war

ABOVE: *Liverpool and Leeds do battle for the 1965 FA Cup at Wembley. After an epic struggle, the Merseysiders ran out victors by two goals to one.*

LEFT: *Scots centre-forward Ian St John scores Liverpool's second goal in extra time to give his team the Cup after a closely matched encounter.*

ABOVE: *Kevin Keegan (left) proved a tremendous servant for Liverpool after being discovered by manager Bill Shankly playing in the lower divisions.*

LEFT: *Manager Bob Paisley embraces winger Ian Callaghan after Liverpool's 3-1 European Cup Final defeat of Borussia Moenchengladbach in 1977.*

FOLLOWING PAGES: *Tragic scenes at Brussels' Heysel Stadium, where crowd violence resulted in multiple deaths and a European ban on English clubs.*

LEFT: *The Kop transplanted themselves to Rome's Olympic Stadium in May 1977 to acclaim their team champions of Europe.*

RIGHT: *Emlyn Hughes leads his team in a lap of honour with the European Cup in 1977. The victory was the first of four to date, achieved under the managership of Bob Paisley.*

BELOW RIGHT: *Wales and Liverpool striker John Toshack, an effective forward partner for Kevin Keegan and later a successful manager with Real Madrid.*

years to manage Carlisle, Grimsby, Workington and Huddersfield. He was appointed Second Division Liverpool's manager in December 1959, finishing third in both of his first two seasons. The second of these coincided with the departure of Anfield legend Billy Liddell, a symbolic act as it transpired. For the following season saw Shankly's masterplan take shape. Centre-forward Ian St John and centre-half Ron Yeats, both Scots, arrived for £70,000 the pair – enough to secure promotion as champions in 1961-62 and Shankly's build-down-the-middle policy was completed when goalkeeper Tommy Lawrence arrived shortly afterwards.

The Shankly years were watched by the Anfield faithful – as many as 30,000 of whom congregated on the Spion Kop, a terraced area named after a hill in Natal, South Africa, site of a battle in the Boer War. The rise from the Second Division coincided with Merseybeat, and the Kop started the concept of football chants with 'Eee-aye-addio we've won the League', an adaptation of the Liverpool skipping song 'The farmer's in his den' and adaptable to all circumstances. Rivalry with Everton, the team separated from them by the length of Stanley Park, was an ever-present spur to the team to do well. Shankly claimed: 'There are two teams in Liverpool – Liverpool and Liverpool Reserves,' but he had also omitted Tranmere Rovers, technically in Birkenhead across the Mersey but in reality Liverpool's third club. Yet it was derby matches with Everton that brought out the best in both teams, and with supporters of both clubs co-existing harmoniously on the terraces there were few more heart-warming sights in football.

From their arrival into the top flight in 1962, Liverpool have never been in danger of losing their status. Their lowest position of seventh in 1964-65 coincided with a famous FA Cup win at Wembley against Leeds. They took the title the following season, with Leeds again the unlucky runners-up. The team at that time contained such talents as Ian St John, the Scottish international centre-forward and now a TV pundit, and World Cup winner Roger Hunt. That year also saw them reach the final of the European Cup Winners Cup only to fall at the last hurdle in Glasgow to Borussia Dortmund. Success in the late Sixties was not easily gained, but when Shankly ripped the heart out of his Sixties mean machine he bought in Toshack, Keegan, Heighway and Clemence – the backbone of Seventies

success. Toshack, the Welsh international forward and target man, combined perfectly with the mercurial Keegan, a Shankly find in the lower divisions. Heighway, a university graduate plucked from amateur football, replaced Peter Thompson as left-wing provider, while in ex-Scunthorpe keeper Clemence the team had one of the two outstanding English goalkeepers of the Seventies and Eighties (with Peter Shilton).

Success followed, with the League and UEFA Cup double secured in 1973, and the FA Cup in 1974. When Shankly unexpectedly retired in that year, he was succeeded by trainer Bob Paisley, signed by Liverpool as a player in 1939 but due to the fortunes of war destined not to make his League debut until 1946! His passage from player (252 League games) to reserve team boss to first team trainer meant he was the logical choice – and the success continued. His initial team talk commenced with the words, 'I never wanted this job anyway.' Yet that first match in charge was a Wembley win – the Charity Shield. And the success story continued. The championship was won in 1976, 1977, 1979, 1980, 1982 and 1983 – but both

'gaps' were sealed with the European Cup. The UEFA Cup came in 1976, the European Cup (the first of three in Paisley's reign) in 1977. Then the Milk (League) Cup, something of a hoodoo, appeared on the trophy shelf in 1982 and 1983 – it was to stay there for the following two seasons too. All that Paisley lacked was the FA Cup – his major disappointment, since a 2-1 final defeat by Manchester United in 1977 deprived him of an historic treble of League, FA Cup and European Cup. It was the only time that Paisley left Wembley without a win or at the least a draw.

In season 1983-84, Paisley had been replaced by another backroom boy, 63-year-old Joe Fagan, but the championship was still secured along with the Milk Cup and European Cup. Fagan's reign was to be soured by the tragic scenes in 1985's European Cup Final at Brussels' Heysel stadium where large-scale loss of life reduced Liverpool's 1-0 reverse against Juventus to the small print. He resigned in tears. Like Paisley and Fagan, the next manager also came from within the club – and an inspired choice it turned out to be. Kenny Dalglish had been signed by Paisley for a club record fee to

replace departed superstar striker Kevin Keegan. Still on the playing staff and with several years' football still possible, he opted to take on the pressures of management. His reward was instant success – the double in 1986 – and, sweetest of victories, Everton were the team beaten into second place on both occasions.

Ian Rush, Dalglish's goalscoring partner, was sold to Juventus, but stayed there only a season before returning to form a partnership with England's Peter Beardsley. Rush lookalike John Aldridge, signed from Oxford to replace him, top-scored in season 1988-89 but was let go to Spain's Real Sociedad. Winger John Barnes, the most exciting British player of the period, was turned from a useful yet inconsistent club player at Watford to a potential world-beater with a high strike rate. The FA Cup semi-final against Nottingham Forest at Sheffield Wednesday's Hillsborough ground in 1989 turned into another tragedy to encompass Liverpool – and unlike Heysel the blame was not attached to the supporters but the combination of outdated turnstiles and the action of the police in opening the gates to prevent a build-up of spectators outside the ground which, though well-intentioned, resulted in the crush

occurring against the anti-invasion fences at the pitchside. Liverpool's Cup win against Everton was almost incidental after that – and who knows how much the club's last-minute capitulation to Arsenal in the deciding match of the championship was due to sheer nervous exhaustion.

The success story seemed set to continue, however, treating triumph and disaster as the twin imposters they were. Glenn Hysen, Fiorentina's world-class Swedish centre-back, was added to strength in 1989 for a reasonable £600,000, while Steve Nicol, a Scot nurtured in Liverpool's reserves after signing from Ayr, was voted Football Writers Player of the Year for the 1988-89 season, proving that even the big names had no monopoly on recognition. Continuity was the secret of Liverpool's success – and few would bet against that success continuing into the next century.

BELOW LEFT: *Kenny Dalglish, pictured during the 1985 European Cup Final, became player/manager shortly afterwards on the resignation of Joe Fagan. His first season saw the much coveted League and Cup double.*

BELOW: *After Heysel, a second tragedy unfolds at Hillsborough in 1989: 95 people died at the scene of Liverpool's FA Cup semi-final against Nottingham Forest.*

AJAX ADVANCE

When Liverpool, much-vaunted Football League champions, travelled to Amsterdam on 7th December 1966 for their European Cup second round tie, they expected to draw; maybe even sneak an away win. In the event, they returned to Merseyside with their tail firmly between their legs after a 5-1 whipping. If that did not silence loquacious manager Bill Shankly, then the 2-2 draw with which the Dutchmen emerged from the seething Anfield cauldron certainly did. It was the first the British press had seen of Johann Cruyff, a cultured ball-playing centre-forward with few parallels in the English game. And though Ajax went out by the odd goal to Dukla Prague in the quarter-finals, their successful path to the European Cup Final two years later underlined their claim to be a growing European force. Teams as seasoned as Benfica of Portugal and the Turks Fenerbahce had to give best to the young Dutchmen master-minded by coach Rinus Michels.

The 1969 final ended in 4-1 defeat, Milan being altogether too knowing for the team – but Ajax's countrymen Feyenoord of Rotterdam went that one vital step further the following year, 2-1 victors over former winners Glasgow Celtic. And though their winning goal, scored four minutes from the end of extra time, was scored not by a Dutchman but by Swedish international Ove Kindvall, there could be no argument – Dutch football had arrived. As Feyenoord faded from the scene, so Ajax's star appeared inexorably in the ascendant. For the next three years, they were to write their name on the European Cup and establish themselves as one of the great postwar club sides.

If the mark of a great team is to win when playing below their best, then Ajax's first final triumph, 2-0 against Greek champions Panathinaikos at London's Wembley Stadium, was rather more significant than it at first appeared. Even coach Michels pointed out that 'Our finishing was at fault, which is why we played a more defensive game in the second half to hold on to our lead.' Only the talented Cruyff escaped criticism. Playing unobtrusively at right-back was a 20-year-old former Haarlem player by the name of Johan Neeskens who, in the next three years, was to develop into one of the world's outstanding midfielders.

By the following year, Michels was running his critical eye over another set of players at Barcelona, his six years with Ajax ended by the lure of Spanish gold. Not that his departure seemed to have rocked the boat: if anything, the opposite seemed the case. The 1972 final, fortuitously staged in Rotterdam, was as entertaining as its predecessor had been dour. Their opponents Inter Milan failed to emulate their city colleagues from 1969 and bore the brunt of some truly great teamwork from Cruyff and company. The maestro himself notched both Ajax goals, emphasising his versatility by scoring the first with his head. The engine room of the side was the hard-working Neeskens, the previous year's right-back, who carried his club partnership with Cruyff into the national team, and the under-rated Gerry Muhren. Neeskens, described by English writer Brian Glanville as 'perhaps the most complete midfield player ever seen', combined physical strength, a competitive nature and a sure goalscoring touch.

Michels' successor Jaap Van Praag rated the 1973 victory, again over Italian opposition, Juventus, as completing an achievement that exceeded Real Madrid's fabled five wins in succession. 'It's much more difficult now. There are many more entries and the quality of football is higher.' Not that Ajax seemed likely to emulate Real's seven-goal thriller of 1960, scoring but once without reply. Like Real, however, the end when it came was sudden and shocking. The following year saw them plunge in the second round against little-fancied CSKA of Sofia – but crucially, Michels had by now persuaded his general Cruyff to join him in the Nou Camp sta-

BELOW: *Ajax's Hulshoff (centre) emphasises the mastery of the Dutch in sweeping Arsenal's quarter-final challenge aside* en route *to a second successive European Cup win.*

ABOVE RIGHT: *Johann Cruyff (right) in full flight during a European Cup tie against Portuguese champions Benfica.*

RIGHT: *Karl-Heinz Rummenigge, pictured in action for the West German national team, proved one of the greatest in a shining selection of Bayern Munich stars of the Seventies.*

dium. Neeskens followed not long afterwards, and the Ajax motor had lost not only its compass but also its engine.

In all the years of Dutch dominance of the European Cup, it was somewhat surprising to see the national team floundering. They failed to qualify for the 1970 World Cup or the European Championships (formerly Nations Cup) two years later. But Ajax's demise seemed to pass the baton of 'Total Football' on to the Dutch side. Their World Cup campaign is chronicled elsewhere, but despite defeat by West Germany in the infamous 'final of two penalties' they impressed observers who dubbed them the team of the tournament. The national side again made the final in 1978, but once more failed to take the final step to the world throne. Their opponents West Germany may not have had the 'Total Football' tag but their club sides were making their own mark on Europe.

Bayern Munich could boast the greatest stars: sweeper Franz Beckenbauer and striker Gerd Muller had, of course, made their name in World Cup action, but it was diminutive coach Dettmar Cramer's knack of bringing the best out of the supporting cast that sent Bayern on their way to becoming Europe's top side in Ajax's stead. Karl-Heinz Rummenigge, for example, arrived at the club as a retiring 19-year-old left-winger in 1974. Cramer bent to his task, keeping the player so long on the training field the coach joked they should put up a tent. The results were astounding: though Germany's 1978 World Cup was disappointing, Rummenigge's goal-scoring part in the 6-0 thrashing of Mexico convinced him of his own gifts. Had he not been injured, he could certainly have clinched the Cup in 1982, but as it was he contributed much to the German Nations Cup victory in 1980.

Bayern took up the European crown laid down by Ajax and made it their own, exerting the same three-year stranglehold on the European Cup from 1973-74 to 1975-76. It took some time, however, for the Germans to exude their later authority. Their first round game against Atvidaberg required penalties to settle it, while an East-West Germany clash with Dynamo Dresden finished 7-6. Even their

LEFT: *The historic East-meets-West game of Bayern Munich and Dynamo Dresden in 1973. Though Dresden celebrate here, they lost 7-6 on aggregate as Bayern took the trophy.*

ABOVE: *West Germany and Holland, the two major forces in European football in the Seventies, contested the World Cup in 1974; the victorious (2-1) German team is pictured.*

BELOW: *Skipper Franz Beckenbauer picks up the European Cup for the second successive year, Bayern having beaten English champions Leeds United in Paris.*

final victory required a replay after Atletico Madrid held them 1-1 in the first of two Brussels clashes. Defender Schwarzenbeck was the scorer on that occasion, but the dependable striking duo of Gerd Muller and Uli Hoeness were back on song for the replay, held a mere two days later due to the proximity of the World Cup. They each scored two goals in a 4-0 win.

The team had goal power a-plenty, but they could also boast Germany's national keeper in Sepp Maier; the roving left-back and influential thinker Paul Breitner (soon, however, to move to Spain), and of course the incomparable Beckenbauer. Their path to the 1975 final was eased by a first round bye, and included another all-German fixture, this time with Magdeberg. Their biggest test came in the semi-final with France's St Etienne, beaten 2-0 after a goalless away draw. The team they met in Paris was Leeds, so often the nearly men of English football but at last League champions. It had been an eventful season for them, for all the wrong reasons: manager Don Revie had departed for the England job, replaced for a matter of days by the abrasive Brian Clough and then the less charismatic ex-England full-back Jimmy Armfield. They sent a defensive side with an extra defender, Yorath, replacing mercurial winger Eddie Gray, but even then could not prevent Roth and Muller settling matters.

Having vanquished St Etienne in the semis that year, Bayern were to face them again in the following year's final at Hampden Park, Glasgow. This was to be their most impressive competition so far, with Jeunesse D'Esch despatched 8-1 and the once-mighty Benfica 5-1. Even Real Madrid were no proof against the Germans, holding them 1-1 at the Bernabeu but falling 2-0 in Munich. The final itself was something of an anticlimax, a single goal by Roth dividing the two teams. But with the exciting Rummenigge now a fixture in the forward line, this was potentially their most attractive team yet. Yet with Maier approaching veteran stage, and Beckenbauer and Muller about to try their luck in America, things were not to get better. They exited to Dynamo Kiev in the quarter-finals of the 1976-77 competition, only to see their victors go down to current German champions Borussia Moenchengladbach in the semis. The Bayern reign was over.

When they returned to the European Cup Final in 1981-82, only

Horsmann, Durnberger, Hoeness and Rummenigge remained from that classic side, although Breitner had returned to take up a free midfield role. Despite the opposition, Aston Villa, losing their first-choice goalkeeper five minutes in, Munich could not find a way through and lost by the only goal. Their European Cup Final defeat in 1987 by FC Porto would have raised eyebrows a decade earlier: sadly, that time had long passed.

LEFT: Beckenbauer inspects four sand-filled dummies used by the club to simulate a defensive wall for perfecting free kick strategies.

BELOW: Leeds striker Allan Clarke feels the weight of a Beckenbauer challenge during the 1975 European Cup Final.

WORLD CUP 1974

West Germany, World Cup hosts in 1974, started the competition as firm favourites – not just because of home advantage, but because of their victory in the European Nations Cup two years earlier. England failed to qualify for the first time since they had entered the proceedings in 1950 – yet their victors, Poland, proved to be one of the teams of the tournament. The attacking flair of players like Lato, Deyna and Gadocha, added to the under-rated skills of goalkeeper Jan Tomazewski, took them to third place, and this despite the loss through injury of the outstanding Lubanski, before the competition their one recognised world-class player.

Holland qualified for the first time since 1938 – and with European Cup-winning personnel of Ajax and Feyenoord to call on their coach, one-time Ajax supremo Rinus Michels, held a strong hand. Veteran third-choice keeper Jan Jongbloed was also to prove surprisingly effective when injury robbed Holland of Van Beveren and Schrivers. Brazil were facing their first World Cup since 1958 without Pele, present in West Germany purely as a media commentator. With injury accounting for the likes of Gerson, Clodoaldo and Rivelino, the accent was on defensive play. Argentina seemed a more likely force, especially with Ayala, the sharpshooting Atletico Madrid forward, having European experience under his belt. Outside chances for a medal were Zaire, Australia and Haiti, with Scotland the only Home Country present. Yugoslavia were the most fancied of the Eastern bloc, Russia having pulled out of a decider with Chile on political grounds. There was, however, added spice in the presence of the host country's near neighbours East Germany. The competition proper had been modified from the usual first round pool/second round playoff system to nearly resemble the infamous 1950 'no final' competition – with one important difference. Four qualifying groups would each yield their top two clubs to a further series of two four-team leagues, these to produce finalists in their winners.

Italy inspired shades of 1966 by falling behind to Haiti before recovering to win 3-1. This was the first time Dino Zoff had concede a goal in 1147 international minutes – but it was also the highpoint of the outsiders' World Cup. A drug scandal, brutally dealt with by the Haitian authorities, involving centre-half Ernst Jean-Joseph saw their form fall apart. Scotland managed the unwelcome distinction of being the only team to remain unbeaten, yet failing to qualify due to a poor goal difference. Zaire were the group whipping boy – and

Scotland managed just two goals against them, a fact they were later to rue. A subsequent draw with Yugoslavia, 1-1, effectively finished their chances. Poland eliminated Italy, once again disappointing, while West Germany progressed to the second stage with some difficulty. They beat Australia 3-0, yet failed to impress. But they failed in their biggest test yet, the first ever international between East and West Germany.

Staged in Hamburg on 22 June, the match was the centre of intense media interest and not a little security. Inevitably, perhaps, the result was somewhat anti-climactic, the game decided by an 82nd-minute goal from East Germany's Sparwazsser. National pride aside, the result dictated that both Germanys should go forward – but the East gained scant reward for their historic victory by emerging into much the stronger second-round pool of Holland, Argentina and Brazil: the West took their place with Poland, Sweden and Yugoslavia.

The East German team could not build on their supreme effort in a group dominated by Holland. Cruyff was in good form, though the

ABOVE LEFT: *'Tip' and 'Tap' were the mascots selected by West Germany to promote the 1974 World Cup.*

LEFT: *The East German squad train in Hamburg for their match against outsiders Australia.*

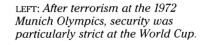

LEFT: *After terrorism at the 1972 Munich Olympics, security was particularly strict at the World Cup.*

BELOW: A grounded Johann Neeskens (dark shirt) scored his team's first goal against East Germany. The Dutch were to progress all the way to the final.

ABOVE LEFT: *Sir Stanley Rous holds the new World Cup, replacing the Jules Rimet trophy, as the 1974 draw is made in Frankfurt.*

LEFT: *The Germans were on song both on and off the field in 1974. The squad record a charity record before the tournament begins.*

119

LEFT: *Johann Cruyff goes down under a German challenge in the 1974 final. His marker Vogts (left) is very much in evidence.*

BELOW: *Vogts keeps Cruyff under surveillance. Despite a first-minute penalty, the Dutch were never able to dominate the game and lost to goals by Breitner and Muller.*

team lacked a natural goalscorer: Neeskens, Cruyff's midfield partner, proved their most potent strike force. Much was expected of Johnny Rep, who failed to live up to billing. Feyenoord's Van Hanegem was inspired in midfield, compensating for his lack of pace by a rare vision. The Dutch annihilated Argentina 4-0, Cruyff bagging a pair, while a 1-2 reverse against Brazil (their first meeting in the World Cup) ended Argentinian interest. The decider between Brazil and Holland proved memorable only for its mindless foul play. Brazil defender Luis Pereira spoiled a good World Cup by receiving his marching orders. Second-half goals from the terrible twins, Cruyff and Neeskens, decided the match and established one of the finalists. Neeskens' goal against Brazil in Dortmund, one of the two in his World Cup bag of five not to be scored from the spot, was a classic. Emerging in a typical burst from midfield, his pass found Cruyff in space on the right. The return was met unerringly, lobbing the keeper for an outstanding goal.

The other group saw West Germany scrape in ahead of Poland, many critics' team of the tournament. Tomaszewski saved a penalty against Sweden, ensuring that Lato's single first-half goal proved decisive. A penalty, this time *for* Poland, helped them overcome Yugoslavia 2-1. West Germany had come from behind to beat Sweden 4-2 in an entertaining game 'of two halves' as the cliché runs, while their 2-0 defeat of Yugoslavia set them up for a head-to-head with the Poles for the right to meet Holland. The Group B decider was very nearly postponed due to much heavy rain. Germany's physical power saw them through 2-0, though not without some concern when Tomaszewski kept out yet another spot kick, this time from Uli Hoeness.

The final was billed as Johann Cruyff against Franz Beckenbauer, the midfield generals of Holland and West Germany respectively. The Dutch had scored freely yet conceded goals too; in Gerd Muller, the Germans had one of the world's sharpest strikers, capable of putting away the merest half chance. The stage was set for a fascinating confrontation. No-one could have predicted the opening, however – a penalty awarded to the Dutch in the first minute. Inevitably, Cruyff was the man involved, tripped by Hoeness. British referee Taylor had no doubts in the face of many thousands of dissenting voices. Neeskens' second attempt was unerring – one-nil to Holland.

The Dutch, however, had the German crowd to cope with, and the strength of their fervour proved as good as a twelfth man for the

home side. Manager Helmut Schoen had refashioned his team after the disappointing results of the first group matches, and it was two of these new arrivals, Holzenbein on the left-wing and midfielder Bonhof, who played crucial roles in deciding the destination of the

World Cup. Holzenbein's pass to Breitner, the overlapping left-back, saw the German defender go down for another penalty: he hauled himself up to score. Then Bonhof outpaced the Dutch left flank, picking up a pass from Grabowski to feed the deadly Gerd Muller. His 68th international goal settled the match two minutes before half-time. The second half could hardly live up to the thrills and spills of the first: Holland regrouped after injuries to Rensenbrink and Rijsbergen, while West Germany were unlucky to be denied a second penalty. Full-back Berti Vogts did a close-marking job on Cruyff, while Beckenbauer, the German sweeper and captain, was unanimous man of the match, strolling forward with authority to lead by example.

The Cup went to the hosts, while Holland had to content themselves with being acclaimed as the critics' team of the tournament. Poland beat Brazil in the third place final by a single goal to leave South America firmly in the shade – for the moment.

LEFT: *Holland's Van Hanegem (left) and German captain Beckenbauer contest a 50-50 ball.*

BELOW: *Beckenbauer holds the new World Cup aloft, applauded by goalkeeper Sepp Maier.*

PLAYING THE GAME (4)

LEFT: *England manager Sir Alf Ramsey explains his tactical thinking to a 1970 England squad before their game with Holland. In that year's World Cup his team could not retain the trophy despite his tactical acumen.*

In winning the World Cup with 4-3-3, Alf Ramsey proved even more influential in a tactical sense than the Brazilians in 1958. His so-called 'Wingless Wonders' started a trend that even now has yet to be reversed. Ramsey had made his name as manager of Ipswich, an unfashionable team with meagre resources and correspondingly few star players. His achievement in taking them to the championship in the 1961-62 season won their manager the England job, though Burnley's Jimmy Adamson had earlier turned the job down.

Ramsey had, of course, been in the England team humbled by the Hungarians in 1953. Their deep-lying centre-forward ploy was one he had noted – and he used it with a telling variation. Left-winger Jimmy Leadbetter was withdrawn into a wide midfield role, pulling the man-for-man marking right-back out of position. This left room for Ipswich's forwards to run into the gap to collect Leadbetter's telling passes from deep. Such was the tactical naivety of the English First Division that this ploy worked unhindered for a whole campaign. In the Charity Shield of 1962, however, Cup winners Tottenham combatted the ploy by adopting a zonal marking system, players marking space and passing opponents to each other as they moved across the penalty area, refusing to be drawn out of position. A 5-1 result told its own story.

The zonal marking system was one Ramsey himself would employ. His most lasting legacy, however, was the so-called 4-3-3 system, first evolved from 4-2-4 when Brazil's Mario Zagalo was withdrawn to midfield in the 1958 World Cup Final against Sweden. The intention then had been to combat Sweden's midfield supremacy by weight of numbers, but Ramsey used his extra midfield man as a chaser and harrier, a ball winner. The man he chose was Manchester United's Nobby Stiles – balding, toothless and small in stature but an indefatigable fighter who epitomised the World Cup win of 1966.

Ramsey decided on his strategy, then looked for the players to make it work. He made his midfield up with Peters and Bobby Charlton, both able to use the ball in consummate fashion once Stiles, 'sweeping' in front of the back four, presented them with it – or, as

often as not, persuaded the opponent to give it away. 4-3-3 was the cause of many dull and boring English League games in the Seventies and Eighties. Without the talents at their disposal that Ramsey had, the clubs simply packed midfield and cancelled each other out. Ramsey's sweeper in front of the defence was essentially the use of a midfield hustler. The Italians changed all that with their sweeper defending the area behind the defence. This essentially meant that any player rounding the full-back was likely to meet a further obstacle in the sweeper. Developed in Italy and known as *catenaccio*, this much-criticised tactic was the brainchild of national manager Nereo Rocco. Furthermore, by withdrawing a player from midfield, the formation of 5-2-3 or more usually 5-3-2 resulted.

There was, however, a positive side to the tactic that had made goals in the Italian league a rarity. By placing a ball-playing defender in the sweeper's position, he could become an attacking force revelling in the freedom of not having a man-marking responsibility. The West Germans were first to exploit this when they moved the talented Franz Beckenbauer back to fill the sweeper role pioneered by veteran Willi Schulz. It was much easier, however, to entrust the role to a player of purely defensive ability, and few teams at club level were willing to risk under-utilising their star player in a withdrawn role.

4-4-2 effectively meant that the players once regarded as wingers were now deep, lying-wide midfield men. Alan Ball started the trend, and many carried it on. It was the death knell of the out and out wingers such as Steve Heighway and the birth of the all-purpose numbers 7 and 11 in Manchester United's Steve Coppell and, later, Everton's Trevor Steven. The unequal struggle of two forwards against four defenders often led to sterile, goalless matches in the Seventies and Eighties. Arsenal won the League and Cup double in 1970-71 with two front men, John Radford and Ray Kennedy, who relied on knocking the long ball back for midfielders like Armstrong and Kelly to run on to. The mercurial skills of the likes of Peter Marinello and Charlie George did not easily fit into this system, though it

ABOVE LEFT: *Alan Ball, the first hard-working winger or fourth midfield man, went on to manage Portsmouth and Stoke City.*

LEFT: *Goalkeeper Bob Wilson shows off Arsenal's League and FA Cup trophies, won in 1971 with a 4-4-2 formation. Now a TV pundit, Wilson also coaches professional goalkeepers.*

ABOVE: *Bryan Robson, the Manchester United and England captain of the early Nineties. His all-action style rendered him prone to frequent injury, a situation that adversely affected both club and country.*

BELOW: *Peter Shilton, a commanding goalkeeper whose dominance of the penalty area enabled him to survive with central defenders of varying aerial abilities.*

was interesting to note that the Arsenal central defensive partnership of McLintock and Simpson were far from physically imposing.

It was obvious the wingers, however deep-lying, would have to inspire more attacking moves. Players like Liverpool's Ray Houghton, a right-footer playing wide on the left, used their 'wrong-footedness' to cut in and strike for goal from deep. Central midfield players had to step up their strike rate, leading to players like Manchester United and England's Bryan Robson learning how to time runs from deep to arrive in the danger area at the same time as the ball. This tactic could take its toll on bone and muscle, however, as Robson found to his cost.

Set-piece moves to enter the game in the Sixties included two variations on corners, the short corner and the near-post corner. The former was merely playing the ball short to a colleague, taking advantage of the law that precludes an opponent from coming nearer than 10 years to the ball. The advantage of this tactic was varying the angle of the cross, changing from an inswinger to an outswinger or vice-versa. The near-post corner developed from Leeds and England defender Jack Charlton's tactic of standing in front of the goalkeeper on the goal line. With offside impossible from a corner, he attempted to obscure the keeper's view – something his height and bulk enabled him to achieve more often than not – while allowing for the chance of a penalty should the hapless custodian lose his temper and attempt to remove him bodily. The secret was to hit the head of a defender moving *away* from the goal, whose flick-on at or around the near post would permit an advancing forward to follow up and hit the net with a header of his own. Terry Butcher and Mark Wright, successors to Jack Charlton in the England teams of the Eighties, both specialised in this tactic and laid on many goals for others for club and country.

The long throw was developed, with players soon specialising in lobbing the ball (legally, of course) from the touchline into the penalty area. Chelsea's Ian Hutchinson was one of its earliest ex-

ponents, being able to turn a throw-in into the equivalent of a corner. One irritating by-product of this tactic, however, was the time taken for, say, a left-back to reach the right-hand side of the field to take the throw, thereby wasting time and losing the element of surprise. Opposition players would occasionally attempt to stand in front of the thrower in an attempt to put him off, but this ploy rarely succeeded.

Goalkeepers' fortunes were mixed. The modern game afforded them more protection that hitherto, almost any bodily contact being frowned upon: the spectacle of a goalkeeper being shoulder-charged into the net was not one likely to be seen after the Fifties. On the debit side, the keeper was now not permitted to bounce the ball around the penalty area, the four-step possession rule being rigidly applied. Rolling the ball was a favoured way around this rule. There was also an increasing likelihood of timewasting being penalised by an indirect free kick. Goalkeepers in the Eighties, like Wimbledon's Dave Beasant, were encouraged to act as extra defenders, even emerging from the goal area to take free kicks. This had the double advantage of both freeing an outfield player and maintaining the offside trap, two players being needed to play an opponent onside. The only way the tactic could be beaten was by either a lob from the halfway line or if the goalkeeper unwittingly directed his kick straight at an opponent (you cannot be offside if a player from the opposition passes the ball to you). No-one called it 'Total Football' – but it worked.

BELOW: *The Arsenal double winners crash out of Europe against Ajax in 1972, courtesy of an own goal by George Graham – ironically the Arsenal manager in 1989 when they next won the League title.*

WORLD CUP 1978

In 1978, the World Cup came to Argentina – a country whose reputation, like its football team's, could use some polishing. The head of the World Cup organising committee had the bad fortune to be assassinated before he could even address the press. Crowd behaviour was an unknown factor, while the country's economic structure, in contrast to the strong military junta, was rumoured to be on the edge of collapse. Belgium and Holland's late bid to provide a joint substitute venue was ignored. The home country's own chances of victory were seemingly slashed when manager Cesar Luis Menotti insisted he would not select players currently with clubs in Europe, where many of the 1974 team had remained after the preceding competition.

Of the previous finalists, Germany and Holland were both to lack their former inspirations. Beckenbauer had, the previous year, thrown in his lot with the nascent North American Soccer League for a reputed $2.5 million. Cruyff, meanwhile, had made his own decision not to participate. Holland could again call on Haan, Neeskens (himself shortly to cross the Atlantic for money), Rensenbrink and Rep, with newcomers like Rene and Willy van der Kerkhof in midfield and the tall striker Nanninga. Germany had new names as their backbone, Muller and Overath being just two of those to give way. England had failed once more to qualify after Don Revie, a great club manager, finally admitted his skills could not stretch to motivating his country. Italy eliminated them, Holland doing like-

FAR LEFT: *The now-familiar World Cup draw, with its complex seedings, this time held in Buenos Aires.*

LEFT: *'Gauchito' or 'child of the pampas', the Argentine mascot for the 1978 World Cup.*

BELOW: *The World Cup opening ceremony, with 'Argentina' spelled out in human form on the pitch at Buenos Aires' River Plate Stadium. The prediction was accurate enough as the home country went on to triumph.*

LEFT: *The Dutch World Cup Final side, defeated by Argentina in an entertaining final. The absence of Johann Cruyff undoubtedly proved a blow to their chances.*

wise to Northern Ireland. The other Home Countries, Scotland and Wales, faced each other at Liverpool, Scotland emerging triumphant. Sadly, their achievement of beating European Nations Cup winners Czechoslovakia was to remain the high-point of the tenure of manager Ally McLeod.

Italy, under the managership of Enzo Bearzot, and France with the talented Michel Platini already acclaimed as a player of the future, seemed Europe's brightest hopes alongside the 1974 finalists. Both faced each other in their first game, in which France's shock first-minute lead through Lacombe was nullified and finally overcome. Along with Scotland, France had been embroiled in controversy over sponsorships and commercial activities – so much so that French players went into action with the stripes on their boots painted out! The French were unlucky to lose by the same score, 2-1, to Argentina with the aid of a dubious penalty in the last minute of the first half. Platini's equaliser was not enough.

Italy beat Argentina in a match between certain qualifiers for the honour of winning the group. Paolo Rossi made the game memorable by setting up Bettega's only goal of the game. Already bearing a £3 million price tag, Rossi was to use the tournament to prove he was one of the world's top strikers. Argentina and Austria, Germany and Poland, Brazil and Italy, Peru and Holland made it through to the two final groups, the system of 1974 being retained. Brazil's draw with Sweden was noteworthy for a goal disallowed by Welsh referee Clive Thomas, who had blown for full-time the instant before Reinaldo hit the net.

LEFT: *The World Cup song ritual takes place in Germany – but with a difference. 'Buenos Dias Argentina' was sung in German and Spanish as a gesture of friendship to their hosts.*

LEFT: *French playmaker Michel Platini, pictured in the colours of Juventus where he ended his career before becoming French team manager in the late Eighties. In 1978, however, his individual skills could not save his country from early elimination.*

Scotland had perished miserably after defeat by Peru and a draw (thanks only to an own goal) against unfancied Iran. A last-gasp 3-2 win against Holland, by far the sternest of their three group opponents, failed to save them. Had they kept a clean sheet instead of conceding two goals to their opponents, goal difference would have seen them through. As it was, Holland followed Peru to the final group stage. If the play in the qualifying groups had been uninspired all round, the two final groups also failed to set the world alight. Italy beat Austria with a classic Rossi goal, but gamesmanship and off-the-ball incidents betrayed a lack of confidence. Hol-

land, in the same group, pounded Austria 5-1. Italy versus Holland saw Neeskens at centre-back in the first half, moving to midfield in the second to inspire a successful fight-back from one goal down to win 2-1. Together with a 2-2 draw with West Germany in a repeat of the previous tournament's final, this was enough to secure them a final place.

The other, weaker, second round group saw Argentina and Brazil both beat Poland and draw with each other. Peru, who had played so well in the qualifying group, had lost to Brazil and now, with nothing to play for but pride, faced Argentina in what was effectively the group decider. If Argentina beat them by four clear goals then they would reach the final. With a rabid crowd at their backs, the 6-0 result was all but a foregone conclusion. It pointed out all too well how unsatisfactory such a system was, and how a knock-out second stage would remove all possibility of collusion.

The final pitted Holland, fully two points clear at the top of their group, against South America's best, Argentina. The latter's dubious World Cup record took another knock when in an amazing show of gamesmanship they objected loudly and at length to the bandage worn on the arm of one of the Dutch van der Kerkhof brothers, Willy. The kick-off was delayed as dressing-room negotiations went on, and history was nearly made in the most unsatisfactory way when Dutch captain Rudi Krol threatened his team would walk out in protest.

Once the game began, Argentina's outstanding individual Mario Kempes notched two goals in a 3-1 extra time win. Had the Dutch had Cruyff, of course, such a margin could have proved slimmer than it appears on paper, but it was not to be. Poor refereeing encouraged the Dutch to compensate for his shortcomings by meting out their own brand of justice, forgetting their 'Total Football' commitment of years past. Kempes' first was equalised by a header from Nanninga, an inspired substitution by coach Ernst Happel. But when Rensenbrink hit the post in the final minute instead of scoring, the tide was turning once more in favour of the home team. An extra time second from Kempes was compounded by a third from Bertoni as Holland threw everything upfield. Though Argentina's Ardiles had not been fully fit, he had emerged master of a midfield crying out for a Cruyff. The final had not lacked excitement, but it signalled the end of an era.

LEFT: *Dejection for the Dutch as Rensenbrink's last-minute miss spells extra time and eventual defeat in the 1978 final.*

LEFT: *Argentinian striker Mario Kempes celebrates his first goal against Holland in the final. A second, extra-time goal plus one from Bertoni won the match in the face of a physical Dutch side.*

BELOW LEFT: *Argentina's squad line up before the kick off in the River Plate Stadium. Osvaldo Ardiles, soon to be transplanted to English soccer, is fourth from left.*

RIGHT: *Argentina bask in the acclaim as their fans celebrate a win by the home country, tainted only by a show of pre-kick-off gamesmanship.*

BRIAN CLOUGH

Ever since the Football League began, the larger conurbations have monopolised the honours. Early on it was the industrial centres of Wearside and Tyneside with their shipbuilding, and Sheffield with its steel. Later Liverpool, London and Manchester put their imprint on the record books. And when all is said and done the situation remains so today: success breeds success. There have been the exceptions, however. Alf Ramsey led unfancied Ipswich to the title in 1962 and was rewarded with the England job for his pains. But one man did even better – and many felt should have achieved similar recognition. His name is Brian Clough.

Clough's achievements with two unfashionable clubs, Derby County and Nottingham Forest, made him a household name – aided in no small measure by his knack of making public pronouncements designed to annoy those in high positions in the game. It was this, above all else, that debarred him from association with the national side – although there is little doubt that his skills at motivation were unequalled. As a player, Clough made his reputation as a strong, skilful centre-forward – coincidentally, a role now filled by his son, Nigel. His career was, however, cut short by injury – a fact to which many observers ascribe his dynamic style of management and will to win.

Another factor in his abrasive style might well have been the fact that national service robbed him of two years' professional football. Returning to Middlesbrough, his first club, he notched seasonal totals of 38, 40, 43, 39 and 34 goals but even these prodigious efforts failed to help the team reach the top flight – the First Division. Clough believed he had a better chance of achieving his objective elsewhere, and made the short journey from Tees to Wear to sign for Sunderland in 1961. They failed to make the First Division by one point, and in his second season with them a collision with Norwich's goalkeeper on 26 December ended a career that, even though it had never progressed to the highest League level, included two England caps.

His managerial career was not to encompass England, the job he himself unashamedly craved, but it did see him in harness with a goalkeeper who never even approached international status as a player – Peter Taylor. They met at Middlesbrough, and when Clough was offered a start in management at Middlesbrough's lowly Northeast neighbours Hartlepool, he tempted Taylor away from managing non-League Burton Albion to become his partner. Things were so difficult that Taylor often substituted the previous week's ball for the new one on the centre spot after the referee's inspection; the ever loquacious Clough provided the distraction. But even though Hartlepool finished eighth from the foot of the Football League and its four bottom re-election places in 1965-66 – no mean achievement given past history – the chairman felt the club could not afford two salaries. Typically, Clough won over the board and the chairman – not Taylor – was the one who went.

Clough and Taylor did go in the end but their (voluntary) arrival at Derby, a sleeping giant of a club, was scarcely spectacular. Fifth from bottom of the Second Division in their first season, 1967-68, they actually finished one place lower than under the previous manager. But Taylor, whose reputation was of unearthing uncut diamonds for Clough to polish, soon found the raw material for a League Championship-winning team. The masterstroke, however, was Clough's: Dave Mackay, the big-hearted Spurs player nearing the end of a gutsy career in which he'd suffered two broken legs in quick succession. Clough saw him as a defensive wing-half in the back four and more importantly an inspiring captain. (In fact, Mackay was to succeed Clough as manager in 1973.) With young Merseysider Roy McFarland alongside, forward know-how from Nottingham Forest cast-off Alan Hinton and Hartlepool's star midfielder John McGovern they had the basis of their team.

The League Championship was won in 1972, in the most unusual style. Clough had taken the team to Majorca, having finished their campaign. Leeds had to draw at tenth-placed Wolves to complete what looked like the odds-on task of winning the double. Fixture congestion forced them to attempt the task on the Monday after a gruelling Saturday final against Arsenal. The task proved beyond them, and the title was Derby's by a point.

Leeds' history is worth examining, especially since Clough was to have a brief and tempestuous spell mananging them two years on. They had duelled with Liverpool in an attempt to dominate League football, the first step of which was a meeting between those two clubs in the 1965 Cup Final. Yet only four trophies came their way: two League wins, an FA Cup and a League Cup. The rest of the story makes instructive reading: five times First Division runners-up, they also lost in the FA Cup Final three times. In Europe, they won the Fairs Cup three times, but even then fell at the final hurdle twice, as they did in the major competition, the European

BELOW: *Brian Clough in ebullient mood. His green tracksuit top was to become a trademark in later years with Nottingham Forest. The former Derby boss is one of only three managers to take the League title with different clubs.*

ABOVE RIGHT: *Son Nigel, a centre-forward like his father, evades a challenge. Clough junior's talents quickly earned him England representative honours.*

BELOW RIGHT: *Peter Shilton in Notts Forest colours. Clough's decision to release the England keeper was arguably one of his few mistakes.*

BELOW, FAR RIGHT: *Kenny Burns, the Scots hard man whose 'taming' epitomised Clough's man-management skills.*

Cup. Yet they were above all consistent: Leeds' league position between 1965 and 1974 never dropped lower than fourth. All this was achieved through a diametrically opposite style of management from Clough's. Don Revie was a cautious manager whose dossier system of briefing about individual opponents became legendary. Leeds teams fought hard, played with a physical emphasis and were often accused of bending the rules to the limits of legality in 'gamesmanship' tactics. Despite this, they had talented players in the internationals Johnny Giles (Eire), Billy Bremner, Peter Lorimer and Eddie Gray (Scotland), Gary Sprake (Wales) and Jack Charlton, Norman Hunter, Terry Cooper and Allan Clarke (England), few of whom cost big fees. Revie's reward on finally winning the League in 1974 was the England job; Clough's reward was to follow him in a job he really had little desire for.

But all that was to come. After Derby's League Championship came the European Cup. Derby reached the semi-finals before losing 3-1 to Juventus. Clough's characteristic bad grace – 'I don't speak to cheating bastards' was his after-match rejoinder to his opponents – was widely reported, and was eventually to rule him out of the England manager's seat. The Derby job was lost after a battle of wills with Chairman Sam Longson. In truth, Clough's increasing media profile (as a part-time pundit for ITV) had been eating into his time, but he believed he could handle it. Longson felt otherwise. The recriminations and repercussions lasted months, long after Clough and Taylor had taken a job with Brighton. Clough then split the partnership to succeed England manager Don Revie at Leeds, where his reign was to be short and acrimonious – the first six weeks of the 1974-75 season. A player revolt ended in the directors' capitulation, but Clough believes the pay-off he received gave him the security to achieve his subsequent success. Despite an alliance between players and fans to bring him back, his next stop was not Derby but the City Ground, Nottingham.

Forest were Derby's natural rivals – and Clough's return to the Midlands was not welcomed by all. The club was and is run by committee rather than a board, but despite rubbing certain people up the wrong way Clough soon made his mark in typically distinctive style. He had reforged his partnership with Taylor, and the good times were soon to return. The League was won in 1978, with the cornerstone a record 23 home games without defeat. Only 24 goals

LEFT: *Forest's Tony Woodcock beats Grasshoppers defender Wehrli as the team progress to the 1979 European Cup final. They beat the Swiss team 5-2 on aggregate.*

BELOW: *Neil Webb (left) takes on an Everton defender during his stay at Forest. Clough made over a million pounds' profit on the England midfielder but could not hold him.*

were conceded all season, a mean machine of a defence headed by goalkeeper Peter Shilton. At the time, the fee of £275,000 was a record for a goalkeeper, but he soon paid for himself – notably in the season's League Cup Final against Liverpool. Other, later, purchases didn't show the same cost-effectiveness, yet Clough had become the first manager since Chapman to win the League with two clubs.

For Forest to win the Football League on meagre resources was achievement enough – but European glory was to come, as well as a League Cup victory against Southampton in 1979. Forest's European Cup wins in 1979 and 1980 were unspectacular affairs against Malmo and Hamburg respectively. They were on a hiding to nothing playing the rank outsiders from Sweden coached by an unknown Englishman, Bobby Houghton. Their goal, the only one of a forgettable game, was scored by £1 million player Trevor Francis, who lent his experience to the European campaigns only to be sold to Manchester City not long after. His subsequent injury record suggested Forest had the best of him and did well in recouping their outlay. Honours were more even in Madrid a year later where Kevin Keegan met his fellow countrymen with something to prove. He was rarely seen in a game where his shadow was Kenny Burns, the ex-Birmingham stopper who even his own chairman had warned Clough not to buy. They had beaten Ajax, the European team of the early Seventies, in the semi-final by a 2-1 aggregate and were clearly afraid of no-one.

Yet Forest struggled after Hamburg to retain their former glories. One reason easily pinpointed was his estrangement from Taylor, who retired at the end of the 1982 season only to return to Derby on his own 18 months later. His partner's spell 'up the road' ended in disappointment. Perhaps the key to Clough's continued presence at Forest was Chairman Maurice Roworth's admission: 'We don't dictate to Brian Clough – *he* tells *us* what he's doing'.

That this was not always the case was proved in 1988 when he accepted the offer to manage Wales part-time, yet was forced to reconsider when the club vetoed his already announced decision. The Derby debacle may well have been on his mind as he climbed down. Try as he might, Clough could not get to within reach of an FA Cup win, his nearest being semi-finals against Liverpool in 1988 and 1989. Forest did, however, get something out of that season, notching a Wembley double in the Littlewoods (formerly League) and Full Members' Cups respectively. Of course, the European ban on English clubs meant no return to competition through the former door.

He continued to buy and sell, as ever with mixed fortunes. Neil Webb, a talented midfielder from Portsmouth, was sold to Manchester United for £1.5 million; Shilton had departed via Southamp-

ton to Derby of all places, where his continuing stranglehold on the England Number 1 shirt suggested letting him go was one of Clough's rare misjudgements. He imported players with success like Holland's cultured John Metgod, yet bought and sold Eire's gifted international John Sheridan before he had a chance to play a full first-team game for the club.

A champagne socialist who writes for Rupert Murdoch's most downmarket paper *The Sun*, Clough remained an enigma in the Nineties. A large proportion of those in and out of the game believed he would have made a better national manager than the recently retired Bobby Robson – a man he has been careful not to criticise in public. It seemed unlikely that as he approached his sixtieth birthday he would ever be given the chance.

LEFT: *Fans are helped to safety at Hillsborough, April 1989.*

RIGHT: *Dutchman Johnny Metgod added a touch of continental class to Clough's mid-Eighties Forest team. The side contained a second Dutch international in goalkeeper Hans van Breukelen.*

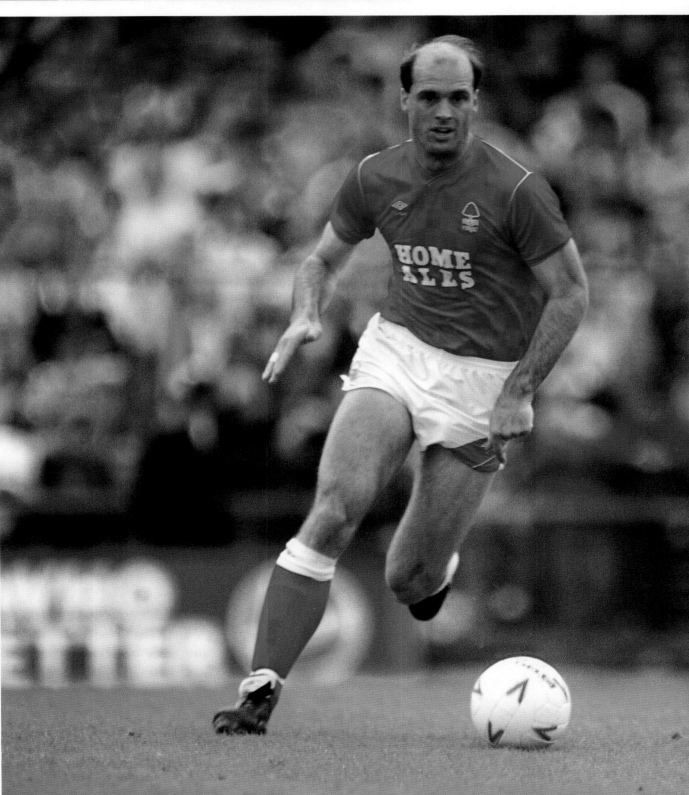

THE MONEY-GO-ROUND

Two main events contributed to the bankruptcy of British football in the 1980s: the removal of the maximum wage and the granting of players' freedom of contract. Architect of the former was Jimmy Hill, then leader of the Professional Footballer's Association, who pushed the clubs to abolish the maximum wage against strong opposition from the Football League. One of his team-mates, Johnny Haynes, was first to earn the magic figure of £100 a week – a figure equivalent to £1000 today. There was a Fulham connection, too, in the freedom of contract debate. Newcastle and England inside-forward George Eastham was set up as a test case of the system with the help of future Fulham Chairman Ernie Clay. The case went to the High Court and was resolved in the player's favour. No longer could the club refuse to play a player, yet refuse to transfer him when his contract ended. The die was cast: the glamour clubs could now lure almost any player they liked by offering extortionate wages – it was, indeed, against the trend that Haynes remained with Fulham. Signing on fees became the way in which a player could set himself up for life, discouraging loyalty and encouraging the journeyman. By the 1990s it was foreign clubs that called the tune, denuding the domestic game of its talents.

International football, too, had ceased to be about pride and more about revenue earning potential. Symptomatic of the malaise was the abandonment of the Home International Championship. Founded in season 1883-84, it had even in 1950 formed a group of the World Cup qualifying competition but its abolition in 1983 was a sad and sorry indictment of the monetary values which now ruled supreme. Two years earlier, the competition had been abandoned when Wales and England refused to fulfil their scheduled fixtures against Northern Ireland in Belfast due to the coincidence of the IRA hunger strikes at the Maze prison and the consequent security risks. This was the first peacetime occasion on which the Home Internationals had remained unfinished, and any forebodings Wales and Ireland may have had as to its future were justified two years later. Ironically, Ireland in that year won for only the third time in the 100 years. England and Scotland retained their traditional Hampden Park/Wembley fixture as an end-of-season moneyspinner for the Rous Cup, leaving the two minor countries to lick their wounds and calculate the lost revenue.

The seemingly exponential rise of transfer fees in the Seventies certainly didn't help the game. The only positive effect this had was that the money at least stayed in football. Many a smaller club would survive to fight another season by selling one or two promising youngsters at the end of a campaign, profiting from the inflated fees while searching in the free transfer or non-League markets for replacements. The acceleration had been fast and furious from when Alf Common had commanded the first four-figure fee. Arsenal broke the £10,000 barrier to obtain the services of Scotsman David Jack in 1928, but it took several more years for the next leap. With Jimmy Greaves signing for Spurs at a 'mere' £99,999, the burden of the first £100,000 price tag fell on Tony Hateley in 1966 when he moved from Aston Villa to Chelsea. David Mills, the Middlesbrough forward, left for West Bromwich in 1979 for £500,000 – and he wasn't even an international. From then on the stakes multiplied all too quickly, and the talented Trevor Francis was the target for the first £1 million transfer.

Coventry City attempted to justify an offer of £950,000 by linking with Detroit Express in the United States. Francis would play winters in England, then jump on Concorde to play an American season in the summer. The bid was £950,000 – and as Francis said, 'there was no way I expected a better offer.' But one came, and the £1,150,000 including taxes Nottingham Forest paid Birmingham for the England striker's services was at then-current levels three times his weight in gold. Manager Brian Clough had reservations about letting his new buy play the year round (something which

Francis's injury-ridden career has proved founded), but since the player had already committed himself to his US club even the outspoken Clough had no choice.

From then onwards, the transfer spiral intensified, as everyone got in on the act. There were some spectacular failures: Steve Daley, an unexceptional midfield player from Wolves was picked up by Malcolm Allison for Manchester City at £1,450,000; Justin Fashanu, an injury prone target man centre-forward, moved from Norwich to Notts Forest but wore his £1 million price tag with apparent reluctance. Bryan Robson, the West Bromwich dynamo and future England captain, broke the £1.5 million mark when Manchester United signed him in the 1981-82 season, after which the market declined somewhat. Champions Liverpool could afford to outbid United for £1.9 million Peter Beardsley from Newcastle, while the same club profited from Paul Gascoigne's departure to Spurs for a cool £2.5 million in 1988, the year after. Not unex-

BELOW: *Ian Rush, whose transfer from Liverpool to Juventus for £3.2 million in June 1986 was a club record fee. He was repurchased later for a 'mere' £2.8 million.*

RIGHT: *Scotsman Alan McInally used a season in the English League at Aston Villa as a springboard to European fame with Bayern Munich in 1989.*

pectedly, however, the club fell into the Second Division for its pains. 1988, too, saw West Ham's Tony Cottee venture north to Everton for £2.2 million. But when Chris Waddle left Spurs for Marseilles in 1989 for £4.2 million, it seemed the transfer market was once again turning the game upside down.

Waddle's desire for financial security was combined with the desire to play foreign opposition – something which would help him become a more regular performer for England than his erratic yet talented displays had hitherto justified. The absence from the three European Cup competitions was having a salutary effect on the standard of player First Division crowds were able to see. This was by no means the first time the English game had found itself in money trouble. Matters had come to a head in 1981, when the game felt the tremors to its very foundations. Business was facing recession and money was no longer easy to come by. And hard though it was for their supporters to comprehend, reputation was no guarantee in such straitened times. Wolves, with a £2.5 million debt, faced extinction twice, in 1982 and 1986. Their takeover as Fourth Division also-rans in 1986 had a happy ending when Aston

ABOVE: *Ex-Spurs and England star Glenn Hoddle (foreground) found the continental game with AS Monaco more to his liking than the hurly-burly of League football.*

LEFT: *Trevor Francis, one of the most skilful players to wear an England shirt. His ability saw him move twice in England for million pound fees, first from Birmingham to Notts Forest and again to Manchester City before moving abroad.*

Villa's sacked manager Graham Turner took the manager's job. Three years later they were in the Second Division, challenging for promotion and with an England striker in Steve Bull.

Not all the stories had fairytale endings. Halifax ended up being taken over by the local council ('Football on the rates', the papers predictably called it) while Derby were rescued by a mixture of self-help and newspaper tycoon Robert Maxwell's money. Bristol City – First Division pace-setters in 1979, 92nd and near bankrupt in 1982 – survived only when their highest paid players (later immortalised as the Ashton Gate Eight) voluntarily tore up lucrative contracts and walked out to enable the club to survive. Hereford and Hull City were other clubs hanging out the danger signals, and it was clear that the League in its 92-club form would indeed be fortunate to survive. With unemployment hitting at attendances in the urban centres, income was decreasing as running costs increased – and nowhere was there a body willing to find an answer.

ABOVE: *Pictured in the colours of Barcelona, Gary Lineker found continental football hard going after Terry Venables left, eventually following his former boss to Spurs.*

LEFT: *Chris Waddle demonstrates his £4.2 million brand of ball control for Marseilles. His transfer brought him financial security and European football, the latter something Spurs were unable to offer.*

WORLD CUP 1982

Held in Spain, the 1982 World Cup's final stages expanded by a full 50 per cent to encompass no fewer than 24 teams. That this would result in an unwieldy tournament was quickly confirmed by a poorly-organised draw. The intention was to keep separate the South American teams, with an elaborate system of drums and balls, the latter being drawn from the former by a team of orphans. Inevitably balls broke, barrels stuck, the wrong teams were drawn at the wrong time and the whole televised event became a costly farce. The tournament resolved itself into two semi-finals, these being the winners of four second-round leagues of three teams apiece. These latter were made up of the first and second-ranked teams in the six qualifying groups. As if this were not enough, a strength-sapping 110-degree heatwave seemed to favour the host nation and the South American teams.

Argentina were still led by Menotti, who had unearthed a prodigy in Diego Maradona, at 21 already a world-beater. His counterpart in Brazil, Tele Santana, had no such luck. The Dutch were unexpected absentees. Shorn of the Cruyff-era stars, they still boasted Krol and the van der Kerkhof brothers Willy and Rene, but they finished bottom of a group consisting of France, Belgium and Eire. England, Scotland and Northern Ireland had all qualified, first and last-named second in their groups but able to scrape in thanks to the expanded final stages. Scotland topped Northern Ireland's qualifying group, but the Irish could boast a World Cup record breaker in 17-year-old Norman Whiteside, the Manchester United midfield man who became the youngest player ever to participate in the World Cup's final stages.

Argentina's 1-0 reverse in the opening match against Belgium upset the form book and the theories on the heat. The teams were to take first and second group places, Maradona scoring twice in the 4-1 against Hungary. Italy played out two draws against Poland and Peru, looking most unimpressive. The Cameroons, one of several outsiders (Kuwait, El Salvador, New Zealand, Algeria and the Honduras being the others) proved enough to hold Italy to a third draw, 1-1. Their goalkeeper N'Kono was snapped up to remain in the Spanish league.

Many teams were ravaged through injury. England, for instance, lacked the midfield skills of Trevor Brooking and Kevin Keegan, yet beat France 3-1. Algeria beat West Germany in Gijon, clocking up only a quarter of their opponents' corners yet scoring two goals to Germany's one. Controversy reared its familiar head with Kuwait walking off at the command of their Crown Prince after a disputed French goal (they were losing anyway), while Germany and Austria allegedly rigged a result to keep them both in qualifying positions at the expense of Algeria. Brazil flourished despite their acknow-

RIGHT: *Outsiders Kuwait threaten a walk-off at the command of their Crown Prince in protest against a French goal.*

BELOW: *Diego Maradona, Argentina's youthful prodigy, strides out against Brazil. He was sent off in this second-round game which Brazil won 3-1.*

BELOW RIGHT: *The silky skills of Brazil midfielder Zico are deployed against Scotland. His free kick was one of four goals scored to one conceded.*

ABOVE: *Brazil's winger Eder on the ball. A scorer against Scotland, he was unable to prevent Italy from defeating his team by the odd goal in five.*

ledged lack of firepower. Their midfield was marshalled superbly by Falcao, unused in the previous World Cup but ideally placed to benefit from a season in Italian football. Their 4-1 victory over Scotland was typical, a curving Zico free kick and a subtle Eder lob the best of the bunch.

Northern Ireland found themselves in the same group as Spain, who reaped the regular host country benefit of some dubious refereeing decisions. One was clearly in evidence when they beat the Spaniards with a single goal from Gerry Armstrong, defender Donaghy being sent off for nothing more than a push compared with some terrifying aggression from the hosts. Armstrong eventually found his way to Spanish football via Real Mallorca. Meanwhile his team were unlikely table-toppers over Spain, who qualified in second place. Italy had been equally unlikely qualifiers, ending the first stage with three games, three draws. Few commentators gave them a chance when they found themselves in the same group as Argentina and Brazil, but both were beaten.

The success story of the second round was Paolo Rossi. Banned for two years when on loan to Perugia after alleged involvement in a betting scandal, he joined Juventus three games from the end of the League season, His inclusion in the squad after such a spell of in-

RIGHT: *Rossi celebrates a goal against Brazil in 1982.*
BELOW: *The outstanding Italian player Paulo Rossi in action.*

activity owed much to his promising perfomances of 1978, but nothing in the first round pointed to manager Enzo Bearzot's gamble paying off. All that changed when Rossi's fifth-minute headed goal against Brazil put Italy in the lead. A later interception restored that lead and a 74th minute piece of opportunism proved the matchwinner after Socrates and Falcao had scored for Brazil. This was the tie of the tournament, with two teams intent on playing attacking football as the world watched and wondered. The prize was a semi-final place, and Italy deserved it, their feat of upsetting the odds due in no small measure to veteran goalkeeper Dino Zoff's heroics.

France (eliminating the Northern Irish 4-1 with a masterful Platini performance), West Germany and Poland headed the other four second round groups, only France emulating Italy with two straight wins. Poland scraped through on goal difference above Russia, with the initially enterprising Belgians stuck on two games, two losses. Argentina, too, failed to collect a second round point, Maradona notwithstanding. The golden boy was sent off for a foul during his team's 3-1 defeat against Brazil. Nevertheless, he had already caught the eye of Barcelona who purchased his services soon after for the sum of £3 million. This amazing figure may have seemed exorbitant, but the player in question was still good value at only 21.

Poland and Russia 'fought' out a no-score draw which gave the Poles a semi-final place after an infinitely more entertaining win over Belgium thanks to a Boniek hat-trick. Sadly, a caution picked up in the Russia game eliminated him from the game, a repeat of the earlier group fixture against Italy. That had ended in a goalless draw

ABOVE: *Socrates of Brazil fame.*

BELOW: *Marco Tardelli pictured in the 1982 Final.*

RIGHT: *Tardelli celebrates Italy's 3-2 defeat of West Germany in 1982.*

ABOVE: *Altobelli scores Italy's third in the 1982 Final.*

RIGHT: *Defender Claudio Gentile and Italy's goalkeeper/captain Dino Zoff display the World Cup.*

LEFT: *The final whistle sounds and Italy are the 1982 World Cup winners. They had enjoyed 'home advantage' by being based in Barcelona, and their 3-1 win was decisive enough.*

– but with Rossi now firing on all cylinders, the result of the rematch was a foregone conclusion. It was settled by two goals from the mercurial striker whose major tactic – unusual for a five foot seven player – was blind-side runs to head past a bemused defence.

Bemused, too, is the word to describe France after becoming the first side to miss out on a World Cup Final place on penalty kicks. On paper, their 3-3 draw with West Germany sounds entertaining but an incident in the 57th minute ensured the game would be remembered for all the wrong reasons. Schumacher, the German keeper and one of the best custodians on view, raced from his goal to floor French substitute Battiston who had run on to a defence-piercing through ball. The German did not receive his marching orders – but more importantly for humanity, if not for footballing justice, Battiston who was for some while in real danger, survived some three minutes without treatment. Sending on a substitute for a substitute also deprived the French of a fresh pair of legs to use in extra time. The match had stood at 1-1 at the time of the incident, through Germany's Littbarski and a Platini penalty, and so it remained.

The extra time double strike by Tresor and Giresse seemed to have put the result beyond doubt until substitute Karl-Heinz Rummenigge put the Germans back in it from short range. Fischer wrapped things up two minutes from the end to ensure an unwanted 'first' of a penalty shootout. Five penalties were scored, three by France, before Germany's Stielike had his shot saved by Ettori. Schumacher, fortunate to still be on the field of play, saved Six's spot kick to level the scores. French defender Bossis' saved kick, the eleventh, proved decisive when Hrubesch sealed the game for Germany in the cruellest possible style .

Having qualified with the gods behind them Germany now found themselves 'playing away' to a team whose games had all been staged in Barcelona. Their worst fears took shape when Italy were awarded a penalty – but with regular spot-kick specialist Antognoni sidelined through injury it fell to full-back Cabrini, who missed it.

Inevitably, however, Rossi opened the scoring – and not surprisingly it was a blind side header that did it. Germany were powerless to hit back, star striker Karl-Heinz Rummenigge being little more than a hobbling spectator. Tardelli's 68th minute goal after Rossi had this time helped set up the strike all but settled matters. With Germany throwing caution to the wind, Altobelli finished off a field-length run from the mercurial right-winger Conti before a consolation penalty for Germany by Paul Breitner. The loss of Rummenigge quite possibly cost the Germans the Cup. A recent European Footballer of the Year, his contribution to Germany's European Nations Cup triumph in Rome two years earlier had been great. Yet for Italy, and especially Rossi, their third World Cup win was the sweetest of all.

PLAYING THE GAME (5)

Holland's 'Total Football' had been the watchword of international football in the Seventies. But what exactly had it meant? If anything can be gained from the expression, a development of Dr Willy Meisl's 'The Whirl', it is the concept of the modern player being able to fulfil at least two different roles, and to be able to do this on the field of play. Holland made this system work by playing a back four, Suurbier, Haan, Rijsbergen and Krol who were all attacking-minded. With Cruyff drifting wide, each could be seen taking part in attacking movements with the midfield men dropping back to cover when required. As the Dutch found in 1974, however, attacking defenders could sometimes prove a defensive liability.

Willy Meisl, respected journalist and exponent of 'The Whirl', explained it thus: 'The right-winger may suddenly fall into the right full-back's place, the left-half may take over on the right wing, and how often do we see the two wingers attack beside each other? Or playing in each other's place or the centre-forward operating along a touch line?' Written in 1983, the words don't quite ring true. Tactical switches by managers (such as Chelsea boss Dave Sexton changing David Webb and Ron Harris for the 1970 FA Cup Final replay to shackle Leeds winger Eddie Gray) are acclaimed in Britain as works of genius. Meisl continued: 'Goals are the salt of soccer life: the more goals scored the more positive is the soccer produced and the livelier the spectacle becomes. Ready-made soccer of a rather shoddy mass-produced type must make room for soccer made to measure by the star players.' When the outstanding League team of the Eighties, Liverpool, carried all before them by doing the simple things well, while players like Spurs' Glenn Hoddle were lost to the English game, while his Spurs replacement Paul Gascoigne could be ignored by England, ready-made football seemed all too accurate.

The sweeper system made a comeback into the British game, with Don Howe's Queen's Park Rangers among its better exponents. One of his previous clubs, Arsenal, won the Championship in 1989 with what was ostensibly the same system of play – but unlike QPR, who had a genuine sweeper in Paul Parker, Arsenal elected to play a third centre-back. This was largely because of a surfeit of defensive talent in England international Tony Adams, Eire stalwart David O'Leary and new signing from Stoke Steve Bould. All were six-footers, and their imposing bulk proved an effective deterrent to those choosing the direct route to goal. More importantly, however, this three-man backline allowed full-backs Dixon and Winterburn to move forward as wide midfield players, moving up and down with the play and effectively turning 5-3-2 into 3-5-2. The overlapping full-back had in fact been born in the Seventies, with Terry Cooper of Leeds and England and Brazil's Carlos Alberto (who scored a goal in the 1970 World Cup Final) the best-known exponents of this 'new' player.

Substitutes also played a big part in modern football of the Seventies and Eighties. The World Cup introduced the 'any two from five' system in 1970, with a goalkeeper permitted among the reserves. Mexico's high altitude and temperature saw many managers attempt tactical substitutions – disastrously in the case of England. It was significant that the winners, Brazil, kept their kick-off team on the pitch for both semi-final and final. The FA first permitted substitutes in League matches in the mid Seventies on the grounds of injury only. This caused some problems: how could a manager persuade a player who did not want to come off to feign injury? Eventually, even the FA saw sense. From then onwards, the substitutes could play a part in the 'gamesmanship' ritual, running up and down the touchline (without interfering with play, of course) to encourage those on the pitch to play to their abilities. Liverpool's Seventies side had a so-called 'Supersub', David Fairclough, a striker who was often brought on by Bob Paisley to score vital goals.

A decade later came the introduction of two substitutes per side, although the 'squad system' was still resisted. The double substitution was now a much-favoured ploy of teams losing at the 60-minute mark, although again it was noticeable that the most successful sides like Liverpool (now under the ever-cautious Kenny Dalglish) could often be seen to keep their substitutes on the bench. Football was now, for better or worse, definitely a 13-man game.

LEFT: *Johann Cruyff's brand of total football reaches an abrupt end in the German penalty area in the 1974 World Cup Final. A penalty was awarded.*

RIGHT: *Glenn Hoddle of Monaco, lost to a British game that failed to appreciate his abundant footballing talents.*

PART V

Football Today and Tomorrow

JUVENTUS

ABOVE: *Riot police gather at the 1985 European Cup Final between Juventus and Liverpool, a game where violence altered the shape of European competition.*

BELOW: *More scenes of crowd violence from the Heysel Stadium. Happily, a special relationship has since developed between Juventus and Liverpool, sealed by the transfer of Ian Rush in 1986.*

Liverpool had been the Eighties' first European champions, symbolically beating their Fifties' counterparts Real Madrid 1-0 in Paris with a goal from full-back Kennedy. Black Briton Laurie Cunningham starred for their opponents. Though the Merseysiders fell in the quarter-finals the following season, the Cup then stayed in Britain thanks to Aston Villa. who repeated the previous year's scoreline against Bayern Munich in Rotterdam. Their triumph was made all the more memorable by the fact that teenage goalkeeper Nigel Spink, called upon to replace the injured Rimmer a matter of minutes into the tie, kept a clean sheet.

1983 saw the third consecutive 1-0 scoreline when Juventus met SV Hamburg in Athens in May. For the Italians, it was keeper Dino Zoff's swansong – the chance to top a glittering career by adding the European Cup to the World Cup he had collected in Spain the previous summer. Sadly for him, the eighth minute saw him beaten by a very preventable goal when he was chipped by Magath. Golden boy Paolo Rossi was substituted 10 minutes after half-time – a move which must have given Hamburg heart – while the German goalkeeper Stein had to be in commanding form to deny Platini and Cabrini successfully for the remaining 82 minutes.

British domination was renewed when Liverpool reclaimed the European crown in Rome the following year. By cruel chance, the venue gave opponents AS Roma what amounted to a home tie, and when scores remained level at 1-1 after 90 minutes and extra time, the odds seemed against them in the psychological warfare of a penalty shootout. But they kept their heads to win 4-2 on penalties, tribute to perhaps Liverpool's greatest ever line-up. Only one other European club final had ever been decided in this way, Arsenal ver-

PAGE 148: *Manchester United and Scotland striker Denis Law, a Sixties legend whose razor-sharp reflexes would have brought him goals in any era of football.*

LEFT AND BELOW: *Two scenes from the Heysel disaster.*

sus Valencia in the 1980 Cup Winners' Cup. On that occasion the English club had lost, but in any event it seemed sad a competition this important had to be settled in so unsatisfactory a manner. Unsatisfactory is too mild a word to describe the outcome of the following season's European Cup Final, staged in Brussels' Heysel Stadium, where the loss of life overshadowed a Juventus win by a dubious penalty. No-one could blame Liverpool players, for whom Phil Neal was in his fifth European Cup Final in nine seasons, for lacking the stomach for the game.

Something else that could not be obscured was the rise of Juventus into the European force of the Eighties. In 1983, they had come within a goal of SV Hamburg in the final: now they had reversed the scoreline against mighty Liverpool. The intervening year, 1984, had seen them take the Cup Winners' Cup back to Italy with a 2-1 win over Porto of Portugal in Basle thanks to goals from Vignola, playing in his first European final, and Boniek. Under the generalship of a Frenchman, Michel Platini, they boasted no fewer than six of Italy's World Cup-winning team of 1982. One of these was the much under-rated Gaetano Scirea, rated player of the 1982 World Cup by Argentina's Ardiles. 'A technician blessed with superb vision. So consistent he never had a bad match.'

The team displayed an intriguing mix of skill and strength. Up front, the incomparable skills of Paolo Rossi, a striker now in his prime, complementing the pace of Polish international forward

Boniek. Between them, making the play and striking free kicks un-erringly goalward with his fearsome shot, was French captain and soon to be national manager Michel Platini. At the back, the less than gentle touch of Claudio Gentile and the defensive attributes of Marco Tardelli headed a supporting cast that, though less feted than their all-star forward line, gave little away.

The UEFA Cup had seen Anderlecht reach the final in 1983, when they won 2-1 against Benfica and 1984, when they lost against Tottenham. In the latter case, penalties were used to decide the issue after two matches had remained at one goal apiece after extra time. Reserve goalkeeper Parks made headlines with the crucial save at 4-3 up. Real Madrid enjoyed a brief reminder of former glories by taking the UEFA Cup for successive seasons in 1975, when they vanquished Videoton of Hungary 3-1 on aggregate and 1986 when Cologne were toppled 5-3. The first of these two-leg finals was unusual in that both ties ended in away wins, 3-0 to Real in Hungary and 1-0 to Videoton at the Bernabeu.

British football had scarcely feared the foreign influence – providing, that was, the 'invaders' from Wales, Scotland and Ireland spoke English. The Seventies saw the gradual importation of players of more exotic background – and though the FA limited them to two per team, some were to have a profound influence. Nearer home, the importation of Dutchmen Arnold Muhren and Frans Thyssen by Ipswich manager Bobby Robson saw them sweep to success in Europe playing some remarkable close-passing football from midfield. The Dutch connection continued with John Metgod at Forest, though Belgians Francois Van Der Elst (West Ham) and Nico Claesen (Spurs) proved brief visitors.

RIGHT: *Polish international forward Ziggy Boniek featured with Frenchman Platini in the Juventus line-up as one of two foreigners in what was basically the Italian national team.*

FAR LEFT, BOTH: *Two scenes taken during the Heysel Stadium incident in 1985.*

LEFT: *Boniek (centre) bursts between two Porto defenders in the 1984 Cup Winners' Cup Final. The Pole notched the winner in a 2-1 victory.*

ABOVE: *Allan Simonsen was one of the earliest and least successful imports into English League soccer. His stay with Charlton was brief and inglorious.*

BELOW: *Tottenham's Argentine midfielder Ricardo Villa takes on the West Ham defence. His spectacular 1981 Cup Final goal will always be remembered.*

RIGHT: *Osvaldo Ardiles, the slighter of Spurs' two South Americans, whose display in the 1978 World Cup brought him to world attention. He later went into management.*

BELOW RIGHT: *Terry Venables shows the strain of management in a strange country as Barcelona take on European opponents. Unlike players, British managers did not tend to travel well.*

Least successful, initially, were those whose skills could be classed as typically British. Tough-tackling Alberto Tarantini from World Cup winners Argentina for example failed to settle with Birmingham. Far more successful were his two countrymen Osvaldo Ardiles and Ricardo Villa. The former, a neat, skilful midfielder, made an immediate impression, adapting well to the English game. The aftermath of the Falklands conflict saw him loaned to Paris St Germain, but he returned to shine again and, after his career was cruelly ended through injury, carve out a managerial niche with Swindon Town. Villa will be remembered for his miraculous and much televised goal at Wembley that helped his club to victory in the 1981 FA Cup Final replay. Deceptively clumsy of gait, he possessed admirable ball control. Another London club, Charlton, signed Danish superstar Allan Simonsen in a desperate attempt to fill the vast empty wastes of their Valley ground. The gamble backfired, and before a score of matches had passed they had lost the player – and soon after the ground.

Managers, on the whole, had found life abroad a little easier than most players. Venables in particular had done much to raise the stock of British football, learning Spanish and proving a hit with the media. Yet even he could not meet the desire for continual success. John Toshack's move from Real Sociedad to Real Madrid seemed fraught with similar difficulties, especially given the club's European Cup tradition: domestic success would never be enough. British coaches had found favour abroad – most notably Bobby Houghton, who tasted a European Cup Final with Malmö in 1979 – but the high-profile appointments, especially in the Eighties, rarely seemed to last. In 1992, announced UEFA in early 1990, teams would be restricted to playing four team members of different nationality to that of the league in which they played. This put a new complexion on the tactic (explored elsewhere) of players claiming their parents' or grandparents' nationality over their country of birth. In Liverpool's case, no fewer than 10 players on their staff would be classed as foreign (non-English), and there was clearly much talking to be done before such a controversial law could be universally accepted.

WORLD CUP 1986

Contestants for the right to stage the 1986 World Cup included Brazil, Colombia and the United States. The latter would have been a brave and forward-looking choice and one which might have sown the seeds of a big future for the game, but this was not to happen for another eight years. Colombia lacked the facilities to entertain two dozen countries, while politics seemed to play a part in denying Brazil. The final choice instead was Mexico, hosts of 1970, despite the previous experience of heat and altitude, and the country's horrifying $80 billion national debt. The 24-country format remained, despite UEFA President Artemio Franchi's opposition, not so much for globally democratic reasons but because it allowed more 'snouts in the trough'. The competition saw the top two teams in each of the six groups of four qualify for the second round, together with the four best third-placed teams – a recipe designed to please most of the people most of the time, since a mere eight of the countries could expect to fall at the first hurdle.

England went to the World Cup under Bobby Robson, like Alf Ramsey successful with limited resources at Ipswich and the FA's chosen successor to Ron Greenwood. England had failed to qualify for the 1984 European Championships after taking five points out of their first six. The route to Mexico saw them in more consistent form, having emerged from the qualifying competition as the only undefeated European country. The altitude and temperature had to remain a question mark after the 1970 debacle against Germany, but the side frankly bore little comparison with Ramsey's apart from the playing formation. They survived a pre-tournament scare when star striker Gary Lineker's sprained wrist, sustained on artificial turf in Canada, was wrongly diagnosed as a fracture. As things transpired, this would have robbed the World Cup of its leading scorer.

BELOW: *A photographers'-eye view of the Azteca, scene of a high-scoring final between Argentina and West Germany.*

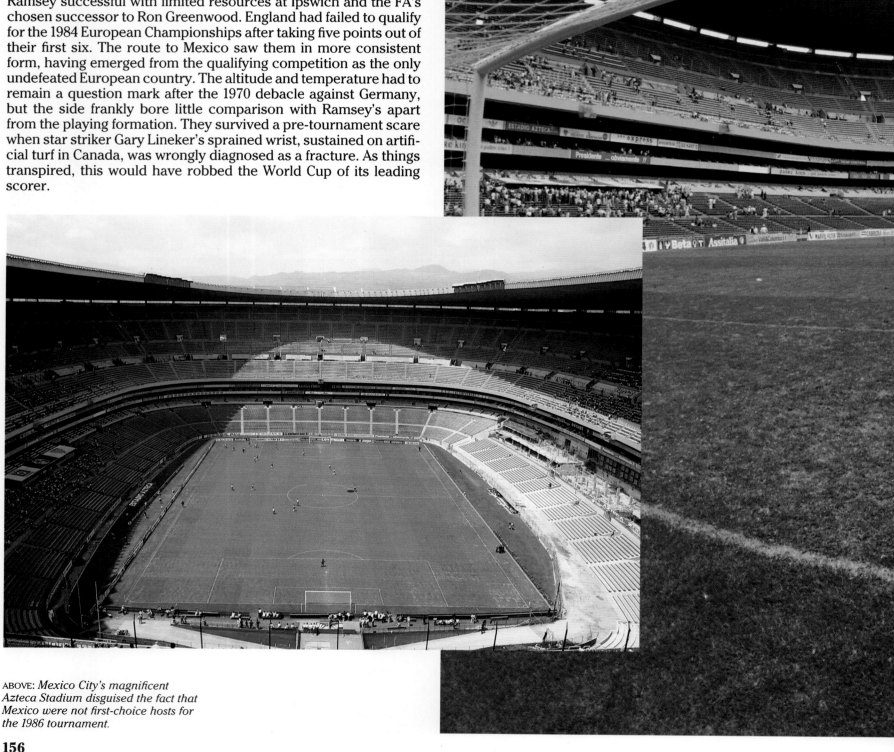

ABOVE: *Mexico City's magnificent Azteca Stadium disguised the fact that Mexico were not first-choice hosts for the 1986 tournament.*

For Lineker and England, however, things did not start promisingly. A 0-1 reverse to a late goal against Portugal was surprising enough, given that their goalkeeper Bento had been threatening to lead the team out on strike in a row about pay as the tournament opened. When a no-score draw against unfancied Morocco followed, things seemed bleak – especially since Wilkins was sent off for dissent. The team was built around the physically unreliable though undeniably inspirational captain Bryan Robson. Manchester United's all-action midfield man was always risking injury in the thick of the action, a 'failing' underlined when he dislocated a shoulder against Morocco. 1966 hero Bobby Charlton made his opinion known that Bobby Robson made his players train too much – and as a director of Manchester United he believed the manager's injured namesake should return for an operation. Robson's injury,

plus Wilkins' absence, led to a reshaped four-man midfield featuring the skilful Glenn Hoddle serving a mobile twin spearhead of Lineker and Beardsley, the latter in place of the tall target man Hateley. Poland, England's final first-round opponents, were the group's seeded team – but a hat-trick from Lineker in 36 minutes ensured qualification in second place. Morocco surprisingly topped the group. Northern Ireland had departed disappointingly with one point in a group containing Brazil, Spain and Algeria. Scotland fared likewise in their group against Denmark, West Germany and Uruguay.

The second round consisted of six first-place teams, six second-place teams and the four wild cards. England saw off Paraguay 3-0 at the Azteca Stadium, Lineker (2) and Beardsley the scorers. Italy departed surprisingly 2-0 at the hands of France or perhaps it

LEFT: *Argentina's Valdano (left) battles for midfield supremacy with Steve Hodge of England.*

BELOW: *Diego Maradona's infamous 'Hand of God' goal, glanced past England goalkeeper Peter Shilton with his hand to give Argentina a crucial lead.*

wasn't such a surprise, their 3-2 scrape past group outsiders South Korea inspiring memories of their countrymen in 1966. Morocco had their brave run ended by West Germany by a narrow 1-0 margin, while Argentina beat Uruguay 1-0 in a dour South American clash. Biggest victories were registered by Brazil (4-0 against Poland) and Spain (5-1 against Denmark). Amazingly, three of the four quarter-finals were decided on penalties, 90 minutes plus extra time having ended all square. Brazil beat France 4-3 after a 1-1 draw, Germany beat Mexico 4-1 after a goalless game, while Belgium beat Spain 5-4 after finishing 1-1. Sadly for England, the only

game to be decided over 90 minutes saw them depart 2-1 to Argentina as the South Americans coolly showed up England's defensive deficiencies. Diego Maradona notched two goals, one of which will forever go down in World Cup folklore as the 'Hand of God' goal for the fact that he glanced it past Peter Shilton with his hand – not , as the referee believed, with his head. The semi-final at the Azteca saw Argentina continue their path more legitimately by beating Belgium 2-0 , while Guadalajara's Jalisco Stadium saw West Germany triumph by the same scoreline over Platini's stylish Frenchmen. France beat their neighbours 4-2 to take third place.

RIGHT: *Maradona displays the art of falling gracefully after a challenge by England's Fenwick.*

BELOW: *Guadalajara's Jalisco Stadium, a venue generally considered far inferior to Mexico City's Azteca.*

LEFT: *West German's Voller turns after notching his country's second equalising goal in the World Cup Final of 1986.*

Argentina beat West Germany 3-2 in Mexico City in front of a 114,580 crowd in a game that, though not a classic final, had more than its share of goals. German defender Matthaus was booked for fouling Maradona – but paid even more when Burruchaga's free kick was missed by goalkeeper Schumacher and centre-half Jose Luis Brown scored. Germany, in an untypical (and unlucky?) change strip of green, had conceded the first goal in the 1954 and 1974 finals and ended winners, but this time their good fortune was not to hold. It was a close run thing: Valdano notched a second but Rummenigge reduced the arrears from a Voller corner. Amazingly, the same tactic worked again, Voller converting a Berthold flick-on seven minutes from the end. It took just one minute, however, for Argentina to restore their lead, a fine Maradona pass setting the speedy Burruchaga away. He beat Briegel for pace before clipping it past the advancing Schumacher.

As with football generally, the World Cup goal trend had been inexorably downwards, Mexico's 52 matches bringing 132 goals at a 2.5-per-game average. Spain in 1982 had produced a record total at 146, but this was due to the fact that 52 games in all were played both in 1982 and 1986, as opposed to 38 in 1974 and a mere 18 in 1932. Lineker had the satisfaction of becoming the first Briton to head the World Cup top scorers. He secured the Golden Boot with 6 goals, Careca (Brazil) and Butragueno (Spain) notching 5 apiece. Hardly Just Fontaine but Lineker's reward was a lucrative six-year contract with Barcelona. West Germany failed to build on a relatively successful tournament. 1988 saw Holland win their first European Championship, beating the USSR 2-0. It was a double for the Dutch, since PSV Eindhoven had secured the European Cup 6-5 on penalties versus Benfica, and installed them as one of the favourites for Italy 1990.

LEFT: *An acrobatic clearance from Jakobs foils Valdano, scorer of Argentina's second goal.*

LEFT: *Maradona once more demonstrates the art of hitting the ground with the utmost grace. His 1982 World Cup performances secured him a £3 million move to Barcelona: after this campaign he was to move to Italy.*

RIGHT: *To the victor, the spoils. Maradona claims the Cup for Argentina.*

163

GLASGOW'S GIANTS

Glasgow had always been a hotbed of football fanaticism. But the return of Scottish international forward Maurice Johnston, once of Celtic, to bitter rivals Rangers in 1989 did more than underline the point. It simultaneously showed, by the fans' hatred, the unattractive side of the partisan divide that linked religion and sport, and also broke the unwritten rule that Rangers would not sign Catholics, and showed the enormous power wielded by their manager Graeme Souness. Already a multi-million-pound spender, this particular signing proved that he commanded the total backing of his club. And that was no mean feat in Glasgow. Managers like David Hay and John Greig, stalwarts on the field for Celtic and Rangers respectively, found themselves victims of not only the hunger for success but the need to be the number one club in Glasgow.

Souness had never played professional football in Scotland, having journeyed from Spurs to Middlesbrough, Liverpool and abroad to Sampdoria in Italy. But it was his no-nonsense leadership style on the field that encouraged a new board at Rangers under millionaire David Murray to appoint him player-manager in 1986.

LEFT: *Maurice Johnston, the ex-Celtic Catholic who broke the religious mould when he signed for Glasgow Rangers in 1989.*

His appearances in the royal blue shirt were not covered in glory – a number of controversial incidents, including sendings off, saw to that. But having hung up his boots he took out his cheque book to fashion a side he intended to be European as well as Scottish champions. Celtic's European Cup win two decades earlier clearly still rankled.

Assisted by the English ban from Europe, he reversed the time-

ABOVE: *Rangers' uncompromising manager Graeme Souness. His arrival at Ibrox in 1986 heralded an unprecedented era of high spending and great rewards.*

RIGHT: *Although initially signed from Sampdoria as player-manager, Souness quickly hung up his boots as he found his managerial feet. He now stands with his ex-Liverpool team mate Kenny Dalglish as one of the most successful young managers in the game.*

honoured talent drain and attracted internationals of the highest class. The money was available courtesy of the huge income from Rangers' development pools, and this policy of augmenting gate money meant that in 1990 attendance receipts made up only around 30 per cent of total revenue. Merchandising the club name on everything from souvenirs to a basketball team and even, it was rumoured, a forthcoming independent television franchise took care of the other 70 per cent. Celtic were not slow to retaliate. Manager Billy McNeill was in charge for his second spell of Scots management, having decided to leave Celtic to try his luck at Manchester City (which he left) and Aston Villa (who dismissed him). He purchased Poles 'Jacki' Dziekanowki and Dariusz Wdowczyk for small fees, but seemed unwilling or unable to go for the world-class players Souness had targeted. It was all highly ironic: for years, Scots had been complaining of the seepage of native talent to the Football League. Now the boot was on the other foot – and how. The rest of Scotland, too, benefited: Coventry's FA Cup winner Keith Houchen to Hibernian, while Rangers recruited Mark Walters (Villa), Chris Woods and Kevin Drinkell (Norwich), Colin West (Sheffield Wednesday), Gary Stevens and Trevor Steven (Everton) and the much travelled Ray Wilkins to reinforce their European and domestic ambitions.

Others came home: one-time Celtic golden boy Charlie Nicholas, after a disappointing spell at Arsenal, returned to Scotland at Aberdeen: Richard Gough, Spurs' powerhouse central defender and captain, was sold to Rangers. As previously documented, Maurice Johnston returned to Glasgow after a spell with Nantes in France – but not to the club everyone expected. The two Dundees maintained a challenge to the big boys, but the rise of Edinburgh's two clubs, Hibernian and Heart of Midlothian, was of equal interest.

Such was the interest and resources that Hearts' Craig Levein was able to turn down a big-money move to Spurs.

Scotland's national team remained an enigma. Andy Roxburgh assumed control in 1986, retaining the title of national coach rather than manager. His appointment to replace the late, great Jock Stein who so tragically died in harness was not widely expected. Yet his quiet demeanour and obvious grounding in the art of the game won many over. There were also the benefits of continuity: even if his tenure with the national squad was to be terminated, it was reasoned, he would continue to hold his post of national coach. As he stood in 1990 with qualification to the World Cup in Italy already assured, there seemed little chance of that.

The future, however, surely belonged to Rangers, who laid down a blueprint for financial survival in the twenty-first century. In 1990, Chairman Murray was able to point to the £4 million development of the Govan Stand and, with other clubs in Britain swallowing hard and reducing ground capacity in the wake of the Taylor Report, a £13 million facelift to Ibrox's main stand was about to increase capacity by 7000 to 52,000. The funding for this was to be raised in part by an imaginative scheme in which 7000 fans bought the right to a season ticket in the stand in perpetuity – a scheme fronted by public relations man (and former player and manager) John Greig. Their overdraft of over £3 million would be non-existent by May 1991, saving them £1.5 million a year in interest. 'That's worth at least a player a year from Graeme,' explained Murray. 'We have to be like that, to be ready to step up a grade when the big European game comes around.' By that, the Rangers chairman meant not a fixture but the much-touted European super league. If Rangers made the transition and swam out of Scotland's small pool, Celtic would not relish being Glasgow's only 'Big Fish'.

BELOW LEFT: *Rangers celebrate their 1989 Scottish League Championship victory, obtained with the help of a large influx of 'foreigners' from south of the border. They repeated the feat the following year.*

LEFT: *In his second spell at Parkhead, Billy McNeill is the man with the difficult job of matching Rangers on behalf of the other half of Glasgow. The Celtic supporters expect nothing less.*

BELOW: *Celtic's meetings with Rangers, always a source of tension, have become even more hard-fought in recent years. A single goal brought Celtic victory in the 1989 Scottish Cup Final.*

DISSENT AND DISASTER

The damage done at Brussels' Heysel Stadium on 29 May 1985 could not be counted solely in human terms. Although football must always come second to the safety of its spectators, the punishment meted out – an indefinite ban on all English clubs – led to a drain of talented players seeking the experience and financial rewards only European competition could stimulate. More importantly for the spectator, however, the Taylor Report of 1990 seemed to be addressing the problem of their safety and comfort for the first time. The May 1985 fire at Bradford City, and the same month's riot at Birmingham in which a fan died, had both led to reports and a short-lived hope that comfort as well as safety might be addressed by those in power.

The safety problem dated back further than that decade. At Burnden Park, home of Bolton, in 1946, 500 were injured and 33 died when a capacity crowd of 60,000 brought a brick wall down. Ibrox Park, Glasgow, had been the scene of two previous disasters: 25 fans had died in 1902 when part of the West Stand collapsed shortly after a Scotland-England international kicked off. And 69 years later, 66 people died in Britain's biggest football death toll to date when departing fans attempted to re-enter the ground only to cause those following to fall on top of them. Not that such matters were purely British concerns. In 1968, 73 fans died in Buenos Aires when burning paper was thrown into the crowd, while the worst football fatalities were sustained in May 1964 when a riot in Lima, Peru, led to over 300 deaths when the stadium gates were kept locked.

Despite complaints from the traditionalists, all-seated stadia seemed the answer after the 1989 tragedy during the FA Cup semi-final at Hillsborough between Liverpool and Notts Forest. That Liverpool should again be involved in tragedy seemed macabre, but the crush that led to 95 deaths was a salutary warning that would, hopefully, be acted upon. Yet even after this many clubs were still only opening their grounds 90 minutes before kick-off – and it was the sheer weight of numbers seeking entrance to the ground just before kick-off that led to the tragedy unfolding.

Yet no League club had dared to offer a seating-only stadium before the Taylor Report made it mandatory to do so. Coventry, who had hoped to pioneer the concept, were obliged by public demand to reinstate a standing terrace. Tottenham meanwhile replaced some of its terracing with executive boxes to widespread wrath and indignation. It was possible that the ultimate result might be reducing capacity, while extending television coverage at a suitable price to compensate for lack of revenue. This was the North American experience, where season tickets alone account for the majority of sporting attendance, the casual fan having little chance enjoying the spectacle live. It would not be the people's game, but it would be a safe one.

BELOW: *Liverpool's Anfield ground became a shrine to the 95 dead after the Hillsborough disaster in 1989.*

RIGHT: *A floral tribute to the Hillsborough dead at the gates of Anfield. The Taylor Report was scant compensation for such a tragic toll.*

WORLD CUP 1990

It was appropriate that the 1990 World Cup Finals should be held in Italy, since Italian club sides had established a remarkable dominance in Europe and the nation's footballing enthusiasm was on the crest of a wave. The Italian authorities prepared for the invasion of foreign fans with a security operation on a military scale. Most worry centered on English supporters: for the first-round matches, their team was consigned to the island of Sardinia to facilitate policing. But, as it turned out, the England players behaved so impeccably that international opinion largely forgave their supporters any misdemeanours.

FIFA chose 'Fair Play' as the tournament slogan and set out to enforce it by pressuring referees into a tough reaction to fouls of all kinds. The result was predictable: a record total of 170 yellow cards and the decimation of teams by disciplinary suspensions. The tournament opened with Cameroon reduced to nine men by the end of their match against Argentina, and finished with the Argentinians themselves down to nine men in the Final.

The system for the Finals was the same as four years earlier: six four-team leagues in the first round, followed by sudden death. In the opening match of the competition, the reigning champions Argentina were defeated 1-0 by lowly Cameroon, establishing this immediately as the tournament of the underdog. Egypt contrived a draw with the European champions, the Netherlands, and only lost 1-0 to England; Costa Rica defeated both Scotland and Sweden. Jack Charlton's Republic of Ireland side, in the Finals for the first time, achieved the remarkable feat of qualifying for the quarter-finals, as did Cameroon – with considerably more style.

From their first match, when they destroyed a good Yugoslav team 4-1, Franz Beckenbauer's West Germans looked potential winners. Italy were both effective and graceful, playing elegant, fast one-touch football, but the home players clearly felt nervous under the intense pressure from their fanatical fans. The Netherlands were the most disappointing team in the tournament, playing well below their highest standard before going out 2-1 to West Germany in a dramatic second-round match.

With Maradona a shadow of his former self, the champions Argentina never found their touch, but scrambled through the rounds with a mixture of luck, tough tackling and momentary inspiration. Typical was their 1-0 victory over the far superior Brazilians, in a game that Brazil might have won many times over if they could have allied more precise finishing to their brilliant passing game.

After a shaky start to the tournament, England forged a dramatic path to an unexpected place in the semi-finals, living off their nerves. A victory over a superior Belgian side with almost the last

BELOW: *Des Walker of England challenges Egypt's Ibraham Hassan. Along with Platt and Gascoigne, Walker emerged as one of England's leading players.*

RIGHT: *West Germany's Klinsman outjumps Colombia's Mubarak. Klinsman went on to the Final against Argentina, winning a victor's medal.*

kick of extra time was followed by another extra-time victory in the quarter-final against an inspired Cameroon. Two penalties won and scored by Lineker eventually settled the match 3-2.

The semi-finals were the true climax of the tournament – and both were settled by a penalty shoot-out. The Italy-Argentina match displayed some brilliant football on both sides, marred by the South Americans' vicious foul play. The final score was 1-1, and the home crowd had the miserable experience of watching their team lose on penalties. The following night it was England's turn. A dynamic England side matched the West Germans in individual skill, determination and teamwork through 120 minutes, only to fail on penalty kicks. The debate on the appropriateness of penalty shoot-outs as a means of deciding major matches was reopened with a vengeance.

The Final itself was probably the worst ever witnessed. A totally one-sided match saw Argentina endlessly pinned back in defence, yet West Germany impotent to capitalise on their pressure. The deadlock was broken at last by a somewhat dubious penalty which allowed Andreas Brehme to give the Germans the victory they deserved. The Argentinians were, as usual, ready to use the foul as a standard tactic, but Germany equally exploited the situation by play-acting. The result was two Argentinians sent off – the first ever dismissals in a World Cup Final – and a game that ended in a chaos of protests and recriminations. It was an inglorious way for Germany to cap an extraordinary record: their third consecutive World Cup Final appearance and their third World Cup trophy.

In the end, the 1990 tournament left a sense of disappointment. Goals were scarce, only 115 put away in the lowest-scoring Finals ever. The competition suffered badly from a lack of truly outstanding individuals. Many of the biggest stars - Van Basten, Barnes, Gullit, Maradona – were either an outright failure or, at least, well below their best. Stojkavic lit up a fitful Yugoslavian performance with his outrageous skills; Matthaus drove the German midfield; Scifo was outstanding in a highly talented Belgian side; and the Romanian midfielder Haji provided some of the tournament's most skilful moments. But these were minnows compared with the stars of earlier Cups – giants such as Platini, the younger Maradona, Cruyff or Pele.

Most delight came from the more unlikely individual successes. Toto Schilacci, a tough, crop-haired Sicilian striker unknown outside Italy – and little rated there – came on as substitute in his country's first match, scored the only goal with a controlled header, and never looked back. Although his skills were not a match for his colleague Baggio, Schilacci eventually carried off the Golden Boot with six goals. Another memorable surprise was provided by Cameroon's Roger Milla. Tempted back from retirement at the age of 38, he proved supremely effective as a late substitute, tearing apart tiring defences and finishing with real power and accuracy. Finally, England's Paul Gascoigne, ebullient and emotional, constantly caught the eye. Not even sure of a place in the England squad two months before the tournament, 'Gazza' established himself as the lynchpin of the national team, with his mazy dribbles, inspired through passes and precise delivery of free kicks. He seemed to hold more promise for the future of the game than any other player on view.

In the end, the greatest significance of the 1990 World Cup probably lay in the performance of the African teams, Egypt and Cameroon. It appeared that at last, slowly but inevitably, the long dominance of football by Europe and Latin America was drawing to an end. Gone were the days when the admission of sides from the rest of the world to the Finals could be dismissed patronisingly as 'diluting' the competition. There is a real prospect that by the end of the century, the supreme trophy would be grasped by African hands.

BELOW: *Argentina against Cameroon, the opening game of the Finals, saw the African team defeat the holders 1-0.*

ACKNOWLEDGEMENTS
The author and publishers would like to thank Advantage for
designing this book, Maria Costantino for the picture research
and Ron Watson for the index. The author would also like to
thank Dennis Turner for his help in preparing the manuscript.
The following agencies and individuals provided photographic
material:

Allsport: 42, 57(both), 61(top), 71(top), 72(top & below),
74(left), 76, 78(left), 82(top), 87(left), 88(right), 107(top),
111(below), 129(below), 130, 131(below left), 141(both), 148,
158(both), 159(top), 162(top), 168.
Allsport/Agence Vandystadt: 151(top), 163(top).
Allsport/Photo:Simon Bruty: 95(top), 131(top)/**Dave Cannon:**
95(below), 108-109, 112, 113, 132(below), 147, 150(below),
151(below), 152(both), 153(both), 154(top), 160, 162(below), 165,
165(below), 167(both), 170, 171/**Chris Cole:** 133(below right)/
Michael King: 155(below), 163(below)/**David Leah:** 161,/**Cor
Mooy:** 121(below), 129(top), 140(below), 143, 146,/**Steve Powell:**
142(below), 144(both), 145,/**Duncan Raban:** 100, 131(below
right), 154(below), 155(top),/**Billy Stickland:** 172,/**Ben Radford:**
123(top right), 165(top), 166,/**Pascal Rondeau:** 133(below left),
169,/**Richiardi:** 75(below), 127, 137(left), 138, 139(top),/**Sven Erik
Sjorberg:** 84.
Archiv fur Kunst und Geschichte: 8, 24(both), 25(below),
26(both).
Hulton-Deutsch Collection: 9(top & below), 10(top), 11(all 4),
13, 15(left), 16(both), 17(right), 18(all 3), 19, 20(all 4), 21(below
left & right), 22, 27(below), 28(both), 29(all 3), 30(bottom 3),
31(top), 32, 33(both), 34, 35(both), 37, 38, 39, 40(both), 41(both),
44, 46(below), 47, 48(below), 49(all 3), 50(both), 51(top & left),
52(both), 53, 54(both), 55, 58, 59(both), 60(both), 61(below), 62,
63(both), 64, 65, 66, 67(both), 68, 70, 71(below), 73(top), 77(top),
80, 81, 82(below), 83(both), 85(both), 86, 87(top), 88(left), 90, 91,
92, 93, 94(top left), 96-97, 99, 101, 102-103, 104, 105, 106(both),
107(below), 110, 114, 115(top), 116(all 3), 117(both), 118(both),
119(all 4), 120(both), 121(top), 122, 123(below left), 124, 125(all 3),
126(both), 128(both), 132(top).
Peter Newark's Historical Pictures: 6, 9(middle), 10(below),
12, 14(both), 15(right), 17(left), 21(top), 25(top), 27(top), 30(top
left), 31(below), 36, 46(top), 48(top), 51(right), 77(below).
Sportsphoto Agency/Photos:Stewart Kendall: 74(right),
75(top), 78(right), 79, 87(right), 89, 94(top right & below), 98,
115(below), 123(top left & below right), 133(top), 134, 135,
136(both), 137(right), 139(below), 140(top), 142(top), 150(top),
156, 157, 159(below).